CARDINAL HAYES

ONE OF OURSELVES

AN APPRECIATION

by

JOHN BERNARD KELLY

With a Preface by
The Most Reverend
Stephen J. Donahue,
Bishop Auxiliary
of New York

FARRAR & RINEHART, Inc.
New York   Toronto

B
H

PREFACE

WHEN it was my pleasure to assign Father John Bernard Kelly to the blessed task of writing an appreciation of one who had given forty-six years of his life to ceaseless and untiring service of God and the needs of his fellow man, I realized that the one delegated faced an undertaking all but impossible to fulfill adequately. It is, therefore, a source of deep consolation to me to find in the portrait the priest has given us a very striking and vivid resemblance of the departed prelate's Christlike soul. Father Kelly has made the most of the rare and precious opportunity that was his, especially in the latter decades of Patrick Cardinal Hayes' life, of absorbing many edifying evidences of sanctity not revealed to many of the Cardinal's associates. I know from many remarks of the departed prelate that he was ever ready to impart to the priest, who was for thirty-five years his disciple, sacred confidences as to his heart's childlike love of Christ, their common Master and eternal Hero.

As priest and prelate Patrick Cardinal Hayes, the fifth Archbishop of New York, was an outstanding symbol of Christlike simplicity. In ministering to those over whom he was placed by God to rule as their shepherd it was simplicity of soul and kindliness of heart that characterized his thoughts, words, deeds, and judgments. As one peruses the pages of this book he becomes ever more convinced that this princely shepherd attained greatness and a place in the heights because he was endowed with the virtue of simplicity which Christ bade us emulate as found in true and immortal childhood. It was his innate simplicity which motivated all the inner promptings of his truly priestly soul.

This spirit of simplicity brought Cardinal Hayes into intimate heart-to-heart contact with the least as well as the greatest of the faithful of his spiritual domain. He was ever one of his own, walking with his people, talking with his people, and praying with them and for them. The almost immediate and blessed success which he found in the all but universal approval attending his labors for the poor, the sick, and the outcast, won for him the blessed title of "Cardinal of Charity."

On the occasion of his installation the Most Reverend Francis J. Spellman, D.D., the sixth Archbishop of New York, in his address, refers with deep feeling to the outstanding virtues of his reverend predecessor. "In the discharge of my office," he says, "I have an example that is near and compelling. It is impossible that I should not be profoundly influenced by the life and virtues of my revered predecessor, Cardinal Hayes. Memory is faulty in many matters, but men that are men remember charity in at least one of its phases—either to be charitable or to be grateful. Therefore it is, that Cardinal Hayes lives in the hearts of New York and America because he was grateful for your charity, and he was charitable with your greatness. More than all no man can give, and the Cardinal of Charity gave all."

May the spirit of kindliness and gentleness which influenced the life of New York's Cardinal of Charity spread like a burning flame throughout the world today, enkindling the hearts and minds of men and nations so that peace and justice and charity may reign again in place of war and hatred and revenge. It is in the sacred hope of collaborating in this happy mission that Father Kelly has written the volume at hand.

It is also our fond hope that the readers of this timely and interesting publication will find in the life of Patrick Cardinal Hayes a worthy inspiration and an impelling incentive for a greater and nobler love of God and a devoted and unselfish service of their neighbor.

STEPHEN J. DONAHUE,
Bishop Auxiliary of New York.

FOREWORD

THE assignment by my ecclesiastical superior to write the life of the late Patrick Joseph Hayes, Cardinal Archbishop of New York, both thrilled and terrified me. The more I became conscious of my own limitations, the more ardent grew the prayer for divine assistance in meeting the call to present a portrait of a man whom I studied for thirty-five years.

Biographies usually make me want to take the book by the cover. They seem to me, for the most part, to fall under that somewhat disheartening designation "tome." I may say in a spirit of true contrition that I do not feel equipped to be chronologist and historical analyst. It was only when I felt that the book might be written as one would write a letter to a discerning but indulgent friend, that I found the courage necessary to meet the challenge.

It was something of an achievement for the first president of Cathedral College to convert a group of young men from an attitude of awed reverence for the aloof arbiter of our juvenile destinies into real affection. It is to me also an interesting example of the appeal which sanctity of life has for the majority of people. In the case of Patrick Joseph Hayes, our spiritual father in Christ, we found ourselves quickly outgrowing our first impressions of him as a symbol of meditative humanity. His weekly talks on Christ, the divine Friend of childhood, youth and maturity, revealed a capacity for enthusiasm for a personal Friend, and a reserve fund of deep emotional ardor. There grew in us a steady realization of his kinship with ourselves.

In the hope of presenting a portrait of the man which would be not too evidently the work of an unbridled enthusiast, I have had recourse to many contemporaries, requesting them to temper my admiration by giving me their estimate of his personality and character. I can say in defense of my own treatment that, after seeking out those who might be honestly inclined to express an unfavorable estimate of him, I found in every case a genuine expression of affection for one they knew only as a public and contemporary figure.

The Cardinal's virtues and personality have inspired in men and women, lay and religious, Catholic and non-Catholic, who knew him as a friend, a similar response. Searching futilely through the records of his life for anything derogatory, I have discovered only an occasional evidence of idiosyncrasy, only an occasional reference which might reflect on his soundness of judgment in policy or action.

As a Roman Catholic priest, permitted to mingle for twenty-five years with men and women whose vocations brought them into atmospheres distinctly mundane, I have found that there is much more heart interest in the eternal verities than appears on

FOREWORD xi

the surface. The masculine half are more timid than
the so-called weaker sex in registering their devotional impulses. But I feel sure that both men and
women have a deep interest in vigorous sanctity
applied to everyday living.

While writing the "biography," there frequently came to me the thought that my treatment
of the prelate's life might be readily understood by
the majority of Catholics familiar with Roman
Catholic terms and usages, but that it might also be
of as little interest to the non-Catholic as a technical
appraisal of a lawyer's genius is to the man in the
street. But my own experience with hundreds of
friends not in the body of the Roman Catholic
Church leads me to believe that the priesthood is a
subject of greater interest, because of its somewhat
mystifying phases, than the careers chosen by the
average man.

It is my prayer that all who study the subject of
these recollections will realize by contemplating
Patrick Joseph Hayes, as so many of us did, the joy
we can have in this life by doing our best to live
Christ as he did. He consciously and unconsciously
patterned his thoughts, words, and deeds after his
holy concept of the Good Shepherd. Throughout
his life he was a son devoted to the Mother of God,
thrilled whenever he heard her praises sung. He
strove to live up to Christ's revelation of the perfection of soul demanded of all who would be immor-
tally happy. The romping, rollicking heart of a sin-

less child he aspired to as the ideal of Christian achievement.

As the Archbishop of New York, he looked upon his See as the Holy Land of old transplanted to the western hemisphere of his day. It was to him the Galilee of Christ, and here he succeeded in administering love to all by inspiring his priests, Sisters, Brothers, and laity to give themselves to Christ as His happy instruments in ministering to the needs, bodily and spiritual, of those placed in their care.

After the example of Our Lord, the Cardinal daily exerted his influence upon the world about him by doing his talented best to be all things to all men seeking peace, temporal and eternal.

When given access to papers and documents recording the priest's and prelate's official acts and personal communications, I found that they were mostly of a character that precluded the giving of their contents to the public. I am, therefore, the grateful beneficiary of data found in a survey of the Catholic and secular press, the sketches in contemporary almanacs, and in such detailed and conscientiously presented appreciations as I found in the Parish Visitors' account of the Cardinal's career. It has been my hope to emulate the scholarly, balanced, and vivid delineation of character to be found in the matter and style of the great Dr. James J. Walsh, who was the prelate's ideal of Catholic historian.

CONTENTS

"The Lord made unto him a covenant of Peace, and made him a Prince with the dignity of priesthood that should be to him forever."

Eccles. 14:5

CARDINAL HAYES

One of Ourselves

CHAPTER I

Boyhood—Five Points

NEW YORK CITY after the Civil War was on the verge of an era of far-reaching expansion in which living conditions were to be bettered, sanitation laws effected, and the general standards of living raised. But meanwhile, there flowed through the stream of metropolitan life a current of corruption which put moral security at a high premium. True, thousands of families lived in the fear of God; mission societies tried to bring about reforms; parish priests directed their energies to parochial schools, while nuns and Brothers fostered in children the religion of their parents. Purposeful lives could be lived in those days, yet it was difficult for youth to stay away from the quicksand of widespread pollution, when it is remembered that most of the city's population was clustered in the downtown labyrinth of tenements, which were infested with denizens of vice and crime. Some of these haunts went by such significant titles as "The Gates of Hell" or "Brick Bat Mansion."

Manhattan Island was at that time the city. What is now Park Avenue was seemingly an endless wilderness, and not long before, Canal Street had taken its name from the water that once ran through the section. A mob of rioting, unemployed sailors, storming City Hall for work, gave the city council the idea of hiring them to drain the marshes which today we call Times Square. It was a profitable riot.

In 1867 approximately one million people lived on the then inhabitable part of Manhattan Island, of whom more than half were foreign born. The Irish stood in the majority, with the Germans running a fairly close second. Along the East Side the latter took up quarters, the Irish occupying the Mulberry Bend and Five Points districts.

To describe social aspects of that old and notorious neighborhood, no statement could be more revealing than police records of the time. In 1867 the number of men and women actually convicted of crime ran close to 100,000. In 1862, the year before the noted Draft Riots, the police arrested 82,072 persons, and the criminals in New York that year numbered from 70,000 to 80,000, a rise of about 20,000 in ten years.

These figures stand out more imposingly when one considers the narrow confines of the city in those days. Powerful political protectors went unscathed by the law, as well as countless other lawbreakers, gang leaders, and members of gangs who continued to operate low resorts somehow able to evade the arm of the law. Needless to say, the political protectors of vandalism constituted probably the worst menace to society that New York faced.

Little Old New York is a homely, sentimental

epithet, subject of many a nostalgic song; but behind the lyrics we are inclined to etch mentally a one-sided picture. Not all the young people danced as innocently as Annie O'Rourke. Not everyone wiped a tear from his eye at the passing of the old Bowery. The John Dillingers, Little Augies, and Waxy Gordons of recent vintage had their prototypes in the sixties in the persons of George Leslie, Reddy the Blacksmith, Ludwig the Bloodsucker, and countless others who ruled hundreds of notorious roosts along the Bowery.

Just off the Bowery, where now stand edifices like the Supreme Court, the New York State License Bureau, and St. Andrew's Church, was the section known as the Five Points, where the Old Brewery towered above lesser brothels, and where for fifteen years the police were unable to quell the bloodshed which resulted in an average of one murder a night. Murderers, thieves, degenerates of all kinds, inhabited the place, despite the fact that the population of the Five Points was chiefly devout Irish Catholics. Fortunately, in 1850 the Brewery was finally demolished only to drag out in its wake the brutal Bowery Boys, Dead Rabbits, Plug Uglies, the Shirt Tails, and the Chichesters, gangs which kept feuding up to the Draft Riots of 1863.

Ill fared the city, indeed. Ill fared the youths who invented a perverted heroism out of the brickbat-wielding mobsters. It is a sad commentary on that decade that the Five Points gave birth to juvenile squads calling themselves the Forty Little Thieves, the Little Dead Rabbits, the Little Plug Uglies. Schooled by their older master criminals, these boys, some of them as young as eight, acted as lookouts, decoys, and even participated in piratical forays along the water front. Robberies and murders instigated by their evil geniuses were not uncommon. Girls, too, such as Wild Maggie Carson, worked in gangs conjointly with young men. Italian Dave, who had a crime school of his own, trained about forty boys from nine to fifteen in the fine art of miscellaneous thieving; after his elementary training, he would hire them out to gansters, keeping an expert protegé for his own use now and then.

This was the Little Old New York, at least in part, into which, on the night of November 20, 1867, was born Patrick Joseph Hayes. This was the American scene, off the East River water front, in which the father, Daniel Hayes, and the mother, Mary Gleason Hayes, in their little tenement off the Five Points on City Hall Place, were trying to eke out a material existence in accordance with the wishes of their God, Whose Divine Son also had made His way into a similar world of political corruption and human debauchery.

Daniel and Mary Hayes were poor as Mary and Joseph were poor. Their flat was made of the same kind of thin wood that the stable of Bethlehem was built of, and admitted the same cold wintry draughts. Daniel and Mary were Irish born. They had left a land, steeped in the tradition of suffering, at the hands of persecutors, and had found comparative peace and joy a stone's throw from St. Andrew's Church on Duane Street. But perverts of Christendom, sycophants of Satan, plied their trades all around the devout couple. Many of these were men who hated the Irish, men whose deeds showed detestation for the Catholic way of life. The couple was surrounded by enemies, even as Mary and Joseph had been surrounded and pursued by enemies.

Mary and her spouse did not hate their enemies, though, and Daniel and his lovely Irish wife went through their daily lives humbly, silently, neither striking back at the foul lies, nor jeering at the obscenities. Catholic bred, they crept closer to the Nazarene couple by day and by night, prayerful, forgiving, and self-effacing.

Imagine their joy that night of November 20, 1867, when, into their cold little room, carpetless, bare of luxuries, there came a babe. The Holy Family had not been complete without its Child, and the Child was consummate riches. Daniel was a poor truckman, but all his poverty was swept away by the first breath his baby inhaled. Another holy family was suddenly complete.

What was more fitting than that the youthful parents should offer to Jesus on the very next day, the Feast of the Presentation, the richest thing they had to give? They brought the baby to St. Andrew's, where he renounced in Baptism the pomp of Satan and was christened Patrick, a courageous challenge of his father in the face of antagonism suffered on the streets of New York by the followers of the saint.

Years later Patrick Hayes referred to that day, when he said: "My father, as a protest against the anti-Irish sentiment prevalent at the time of my birth, determined to call his first-born, Patrick."

Patrick Hayes played with his comrades in those narrow streets and breathed the heavy air. He had a wiry thinness in his small frame and a huge capacity for the excitement and fun of "Cops and Robbers," "I Spy the Woolly Woolly Wolf," "Prisoner's Base," and other pastimes which made up his daily diversions. Often he stood off to the side watching. He was not a sickly or frail boy, though he lacked brawn. While cheering his side in the game, he would notice urchins of the neighborhood making their way through the crowded lanes. They were dark, swarthy lads with the glint of cunning men in their hard young eyes. Their game was Crime; their heroes, the gang leaders who employed them. Patrick Joseph noticed that they crept rather than walked.

Suddenly, when Patrick was four years old, his mother died. A void was left both in the heart of Daniel and in the life of the little boy. The father was full of common sense and wisdom. He was also full of the spirit of St. Joseph. Joseph had wasted no time in conveying the Child in his care to a place where He could grow and develop under conditions of peace and enjoyment. Daniel Hayes brought Patrick to the home of his deceased wife's sister, Ellen Egan.

Ellen and Jim Egan were childless. Thus did little Patrick, for the second time, bring riches into the lives of a couple whom the world numbered among its poor. The Egans had lived in a tenement flat, but although hampered by comparative poverty, they did not stoop to slovenliness. Uncle Jim and Aunt Ellen and their foster son were, nevertheless, not entirely friendless.

Inside the Egan flat little Patrick listened to Aunt Ellen's story of the Christ Child skipping about the carpenter shop, carrying nails to Joseph, sweeping out the sawdust. He smiled as the narrative lengthened. Mary was in that story, Mary and Joseph and the Boy, having gay fun together as they did the day's chores.

Once in a while Aunt Ellen would glance sidelong at Patrick. His eyes gleamed. Uncle Jim, relaxing in a chair, lids closed, followed the tale until time came for the three to recite the Rosary. "Hail Mary, full of grace, the Lord is with thee . . . And blessed is the fruit of thy womb, Jesus."

In a distance a tinny piano clinked a tinny tune. Voices lifted to a vulgar pitch, vainly trying to sing in harmony. The attempt broke off in a sudden cackle, followed by hysterical laughter.

But the Egans went to bed, simple, unpreten-

tious. There was no piano in their parlor. Nobody
had come in to sing or dance. Nobody had been
there with them, nobody except the Holy Family.

Patrick had just been graduated from the parochial school in St. James' parish, and he was thinking back to the events that were recorded in his
mind's diary. Rising earlier than usual, he had been
assisted by his second mother, Aunt Ellen Egan, to
dress for the function which was to be staged in the
school assembly room. Everything he wore had the
feeling of being brand new—underwear, stockings,
shirt, suit, and patent leather shoes that crinkled
and glistened as he walked. He had rehearsed the
little piece he was to recite. He had walked up to
the great man who was giving out the diplomas,
after uttering a serious pronouncement on what
boys should grow up to be as men.

The boy Patrick was distressed about the contrast between the urchins who darted up alleys and
himself. Their thoughts were not his thoughts, he
was sure. He heard their jargon and knew they did
not speak as he and the boys from St. James' School
spoke. Their eyes were shifty, and he shuddered to
think of the fear in which they lived. He was as poor
as they, but their clothes, dirty, unmended, did
not know the loving hands of an Aunt Ellen. She
always told Patrick that cleanliness was next to godliness; and he felt sorry for these other little fellows.
Cleanliness is next to godliness. Many were not

taught to be clean inside; how could they be clean outside?

Long years after, in an address to the Grand Street Boys, Cardinal Hayes reflected on the days of his boyhood. The old downtown neighborhood in which he had lived did not take on any sordidness in his description, for it was like him to remember only the best about things and people.

"Let me turn back to Grand Street," he said in his address. "I can see it now as I did forty years ago. To you and to me it was then the top of the earth. The great city we have today is, after all, but an expansion of what we found on the dear old highway. There was the Board of Education at one end, typical of New York's care of children; at the other end the old ferry which so often carried across the river to God's acre our sacred dead; transportation was then a problem as it is today; the various lines of street-cars converged to, and radiated from the old street; the impressive foundry and printing press establishment; the merchants and shopkeepers then marking the beginning of departmental stores— all this and much more gave to the old street and neighborhood a grandeur all its own. May this memory live long in our hearts!"

But that day when, as a boy, the realization came upon him of the difference between himself and the unfortunate urchins he had seen in the street, he walked home slowly. He felt peace and happiness within him; yet there was a shadow, as on the day his father had died. He was happy that day only because he still had Aunt Ellen and Uncle Jim. He was sorry because he had lost something. Now he wanted to go home where they were, wishing he could take the Little Plug Uglies with him. They needed what he had, poor grimy little fellows, snatching food from stands and running, proud that they could get away with their petty loot. They had no Aunt Ellen to wash them; no Uncle Jim to teach them to be gentlemen. No one was kind to them; and so they didn't know how to be kind.

Most of all he was sorry for them because they had no real hero. Now, the heroes of American boyhood seventy years ago were chiefly, as they are to-day, national figures of conquest, statesmanship and sports. All of us sometimes forget that elegant externals do not make a man a hero, any more than a soldier's uniform made Stonewall Jackson a soldier.

Patrick remembered everything that had happended a few days before. The boys had been hearing stories about Washington, Sir Walter Raleigh, and other famous men. Their deeds made them heroes in the boys' eyes. They talked about heroes in general and what it took to be a hero.

"Aw, what's the use of talkin' about it?" asked one. "Ya gotta have a lotta money to be a hero."

"Yeah, that's right. Ya hafta be rich and have boats," injected another.

"An' swords, and soldiers to yell 'Charge!' to,

and they charge!" yelled a third, raising his arm and waving it with a mighty sweep, as he envisioned his men ready for the command.

The first lad hitched up his trousers, hunching one shoulder and then the other, thinking of the impression he was making. He was in the eighth grade in the public school on Duane Street and fancied himself well up on history.

Patrick heard these ideas being passed around, but remained silent.

"Sure," the leader said, "you can't just live in a back alley and eat stew every night o' the week. Ya gotta get out in the world. Ya gotta wear velvet coats. All the big men had swords, too. And had their names in books."

"Look at Napoleon!" cried someone. "He wore gold ropes all over him!"

The group was breaking up. They were not all Catholics. The boy next to Patrick looked glum. Patrick said to him quietly, "You don't even have to be grown up to be a hero. A boy can be a hero."

The other peered at him with squinted eyes. "A poor boy can live in a shack and be great," Patrick continued.

Suddenly his companion gave a shout. "Hey, fellas! Hayes says a *kid* can be a hero!" The group moved around the two. They stared at him, waiting for him to explain.

"Jesus was a poor Boy!" he said calmly and

started away. Behind him he heard disparaging remarks, but he had noted some thoughtful faces as
he turned out of the circle.

The significance of this incident must be understood, in order to understand Patrick Hayes, the
Cardinal. To get a real picture of a man it is first
necessary to know who his heroes were as life developed. And then it is necessary to find how he followed those heroes throughout his life. To emulate
a hero requires courage. To do so openly and in a
society that does not believe in your hero is the first
step in the making of another hero.

Once Aunt Ellen was asked by her little
nephew how it was that people could live through
"awful times." He had heard talk of awful times.
She answered: "Mary and Joseph lived through the
reign of Herod and the slaughter of the Holy Innocents."

He understood enough of the world from his
own humble surroundings to know that not everyone was happy. He recognized that many of the
poor hated their poverty. But he had a clear picture
of the poverty of the Holy Family. Jesus was part
of that Family, and Jesus was his friend. He wanted
to be like Him, near Him, liked by Him. Jesus was
his Hero. The essence of a hero is that he can do no
wrong, and if his Hero loved the poor, he, Patrick,
would love them too. As his Hero loved His ene-

mies, so must he, Patrick, love those at whom the world looks askance.

Churches in that old downtown area were oases in a desert—few and far between. Yet Cardinal Hayes referred afterwards to Five Points as "A section of the metropolis in which we were born and played; went to school; prayed and even toiled, perhaps, at a tender age; where our humble homes were with father and mother, brother and sister; where friendships were formed to be made sacred for life by marriage, and others by companionship that even the lengthening years could not sever. The nobility of any man suffers when he fails to remember the pit from which he was dug and the clay from which he was formed."

While still in the early grades of grammar school Patrick became an altar boy at St. Andrew's. In the cold gray of winter dawns he slid across icy streets to don cassock and surplice. His hands were often numb as they held the taper to light the Mass candles. But he enjoyed everything that went with his duties as assistant. Life was always a tremendous game for him and serving Mass was part of the adventure.

He learned a simple phrase, and the phrase became a formula: "I will go in unto the altar of God: unto God Who giveth joy to my youth!" Kneeling at the altar each morning, he said these words over and over. Joy and youth! Youth was the game of life and he had to play it, he felt, with all his zeal for doing joyful things. He did not have to serve Mass; he did it because in this way he was becoming a closer comrade to his Friend, Jesus. In his mind as a boy he relived the drama of Christ's life. He never tired of harking back to Five Points. He once remarked: "May it prove a symbol in these later years of our lives or a noble sentiment of friendly and loyal attachment to the cradle that bore us, to the playground that made us happy, to the school that taught us, to the synagogue or church wherein we worshipped, to the shop or store we labored in, and finally, to the friends who made our early days happy, and our later days successful."

No artist was needed to make graphic to the boy, Patrick, the early life of Christ, as the Boy, Who, at twelve years of age had sat in academic discourse with the Jewish elders. Patrick Hayes could see the faces of those old scholars, eyes wide, bodies tense, minds straining to follow the logic of a Boy. The lesson over, Jesus rose to greet Mary and Joseph. His auditors were spent with wonderment after the three-day interview.

Whenever Patrick Joseph Hayes came to this part of the story, his whole body became warm. This was one of the most gripping of all the stories of his boyhood. It was like a success story that one might read in school, except that this one about Jesus talking with the elders in the Temple was true. Too much of his other reading was mere fable and fiction!

Patrick Hayes never dramatized himself, as so many boys are inclined to do. He inhaled the city air, purged of its dust and smoke by salty gusts driven in from the harbor. His lungs swelled to receive them and he felt himself strong. His was no puny asceticism, even if he did go to serve Mass every morning.

The poverty of Five Points was Patrick Hayes' cradle of sanctity. This is the paradox of his life. He was a poor boy; an orphan at the age of six. The world's goods could have been his if he had walked a few short streets up the Bowery and thrown his tattered cap into the lap of the Fagins. Instead, he tossed it into the stable of Bethlehem. He hugged the stable straw to his breast. It was the wellspring of his virtue.

CHAPTER II

Schooldays

MANY men and women in all sincerity consider friends or acquaintances who choose to give their lives to the service of God in religious communities as either mysterious or eccentric. They cannot fathom the reasoning that prompts hale, hearty, up-and-doing young men and women to embrace religion as a career which separates them largely from the vital interests of their old friends. Some men, and women too, look upon the young man who has shown marked talents for success in current professions, or in the sphere of business, as abnormal, when he quietly draws aside from the interests and routine of his companions to seek a place in a religious Order or in an environment that cuts him off from former associations. Some see him as a victim of self-nurtured emotions that are a contradiction of the normal ambitions and aspirations of manhood. Some see the masculine or feminine aspirant to the religious life as following with stubborn fortitude a resolve that can be traced to "disappointment in love." It is to these honest self-deluders that the life of Patrick Hayes should be a revealing study.

There are photographs of the youth at the ages

of sixteen and seventeen in the possession of his family, and in the records of the ecclesiastical officials surviving him. Physically he was of the type that very often outlives the more bodily robust. He was rather fair in complexion, and had blue eyes that mirrored a soul interested in most things appealing to his contemporaries, but there was nothing to suggest the brooder in their habitual focus upon a world beyond that immediately visible. He had little or no inclination to initiate or participate in the boisterous deeds and declamations characteristic of ebullient youth, but neither was there any frown of disapproval for his classmates' lapses into hilarity or innocent buffoonery. The heart of Patrick Hayes, the youth, was singing a hymn of gladness, which had for its theme the first words of the Latin tongue he was given to memorize as an altar boy in the parish church: "I will go in unto the altar of God: unto God who giveth joy to my youth!"

The devoted Egans were studying their protégé with eager interest, but both wore a mask of apathy as to the lad's choice of religious service as his life-work. There is in Roman Catholic parents a sense of absolute, moral obligation to abstain from any thought, word or deed that might be an invasion of the inviolable and sole prerogative of Christ to choose His disciples from among His subjects eligible to position in the religious life. "You have not chosen Me. I have chosen you," is His vividly remembered dictum. The candidate called into His service can withhold consent, but he cannot intrude upon the banquet of the élite, spread for those divinely invited to participate. The fate of the man without the wedding garment awaits the unsummoned invader of the Host's sacred precincts.

Patrick Hayes, at the age of sixteen, was inclined to be pensive, but he was not in any way unsociable. In the year 1883 he found himself among young men, in De La Salle Institute in Second Street, who were in the initial stage of preparation for their chosen careers. The Egans had chosen to deprive themselves of all luxuries enjoyed by their neighbors of similar circumstances, in order to arrange for their ward's entrance into the first period of higher education. Their reliance upon the Christian Brothers to nurture vocations to the secular or religious life gave them peace of soul and full compensation for their self-sacrificing investment in tuition expenses. The Brothers were of an Order wealthy in accumulated experience in the training of youth.

The lasting value of his early schooling under these patrons, and his appreciation of the influence of the Christian Brothers on his development, prompted Patrick Cardinal Hayes years later to encourage others to value and appreciate their training received in Catholic schools: "When you go out from your studies, be loyal to your school and say a word for the modern knight, the layman of the Church, whose one purpose is to implant faith in the hearts of all, that God may reign. All Catholics understand the work of the priest; they know him through the Mass and the sacramental ministrations. Comparatively few come to know the lives and the ideals of the religious teacher. Could they but realize the vital contribution made by the Brother and Sister to Catholic education, and therefore to Catholic life, they would be far more zealous to promote and pray for these special vocations."

The Brothers at De La Salle were intolerant of any mollycoddling influence in their system of training their pupils. Courage was, and is, to them the primary requirement for success in a world challenging aspiration and idealism in its dependents. They placed vividly before their students the uncompromising valor of history's true heroes, who surmounted all obstacles. To this end they engendered in their students a legitimate ambition to conquer rival teams and personal competitors for honors of the athletic arena.

Patrick Hayes was one with his classmates in enthusiasm for these periods of recreation, but he was not a participant in interclass or interschool events of the athletic arena. He was the cheer leader rooting for his fellows, or acting as arbiter of disputed decisions. His own form of exercise was walking with congenial spirits ready to discuss current interests in the school's curriculum. His mind was focused on the figures of history presented by his tutors and text books. He measured these men and women by the standard of altruism applied by their sayings and deeds, after comparing their stature with Christ's revealed norm of greatness. Christ was his study and ever-present Ideal, in his subconsciousness as well as in the hours given to the greatest of all stories, New Testament's inspired narrative. As he fingered the fifteen decades of the Rosary, telling in as many chapters the story of Mary's heroism and exalted place through devotion to her Son and God, he called upon her in prayer to help him become another Christ, ready, by the grace of God, to re-enact the Master's heroism, from the cradle to the throne of eternal triumph. She whispered to him that her divine Child was his own personal possession, given him to have and to hold, on the day of his first Holy Communion and on each reception of the Host since then.

The opportunity for adventure, provided by the assignments given to Roman Catholic priests, was a thrilling study to him as he pored over the records of men who set out in relatively frail barks to find new lands in which to tell strange people the wonderful story of Christ's majesty and humility. Memories of youth's dreams found expression when he said later, at a dedication in the rural districts of his archdiocese: "Catholic America has every reason to rejoice . . . because over our beloved land, since its discovery four centuries ago by a Catholic navigator, has hovered and spread the benediction of our Blessed Savior in the Sacrifice and Sacrament of the Holy Eucharist." He went on to say, "The pioneer missioners, the Dominicans, Franciscans, and Jesuits, who played so valuable and prominent a part in the opening up of this continent to civilization, were, above all else, apostles, bearers and ministers of the Holy Eucharist. Like Elias of old, who was nourished by an angel with bread in his journey to Mount Horeb, these heroic priests of God found in the Blessed Sacrament 'that sacrifice from which all martyrdom has drawn its source,' the mighty spirit of their courage, of their endurance, of their boundless privations, and even for many of them the superhuman strength to suffer savage torture and the cruelest of deaths."

He was indeed a happy youth when his loyal patrons, the Egans, told him they would contrive to meet his expenses at Manhattan College. He saw himself privileged to continue his studies under the tutelage of the same body of men who had opened up for him worlds of fascinating interest, as they revealed to him principles of science, applied doctrines in mathematical research, the beauty and utility of languages, correct usages in speaking and writing the English tongue, and the sources of Christian apologetics that confirmed the faith inherited largely from the older folks at home.

On June 2, 1932, His Eminence presided at the seventy-ninth annual commencement exercises of Manhattan College, the "College of Cardinals," called such by reason of the fact that it is the alma mater of two Americans who became Princes of the Church after their graduation. (The other Prince of the Church who received his degree from Manhattan College is Cardinal Mundelein of Chicago. God rest his soul!)

Addressing the graduates and guests at the close of the program, His Eminence said: "It is a special gratification to me to realize that my alma mater is today sending out the largest graduating class in its history. This is indeed an evidence of progress. These boys who are graduating today cannot realize the difference between their Manhattan and the Manhattan of my day. The old Manhattan perhaps would not be fine enough or elegant enough for some of the graduates of today, but it has been said that the old Manhattan got along quite splendidly, and, oh, what a love and affection those of us who were students at old Manhattan had for our alma mater! My prayer is that you will carry away with you that same love for Manhattan."

It was in the home that he found an education in loyalty to the truths of the Apostle's Creed—a loyalty born of the conviction that there must be specialists with authority and right to speak in matters vital to humanity's eternal salvation, just as positively as the physicians, lawyers, and statesmen, upon whose knowledge and honesty the average man and woman rely in life's crises.

Patrick Hayes could not have been much more content had he been in the home of his father and

mother instead of in the simple domicile of the
Egans, who found the joy of fatherhood and motherhood in their common love of, and devotion to, the
young man who was the perpetuation of the
decency, charm, and vigor of loyalty to God and
country that were so deeply imbedded in his departed parents. They both found his contentment
of heart a source of peace in their own common
lives. They felt that his trust in them was life's richest reward. Their joy grew as they sensed in his
words and actions a bent to develop the devotional
in his religious exercises. They were uncompromising in their leaving his choice of life's vocation to
his own self-determination. They frequently suggested to him the professions of law, medicine, commerce, and engineering. Nevertheless, their prayers
in sacredly guarded silence were that he might make
the priesthood his choice, even as they courageously
stated the bright promises of a secular career.

The youth was, with secret aspiration, praying
for a vocation to the service of God as one of His
ministers. The primary source of life's happiness
he found in studying Christ in the priests of his
acquaintance. He saw them as men who were ready
to smile and exchange a bit of comedy like his
friends and acquaintances outside the priesthood.
He saw them as men as much interested in the news
of the day as were their fellows in trades and professions. There was no gloom in their manner. Those
who thundered out their disappointments, found in

humanity's shortcomings, were in a marked minority. Patrick Hayes' teachers in prep school and college were carefully scrutinized by this young man, and his scrutiny found them ever ready to acknowledge the reverence due the cloth—not because of any remarkable endowments of personal charm or intellectual talent, but because they were empowered to act for Christ in dispensing the gifts of life and light that God alone can bestow. They had the power to raise a man from the state of death eternal, more commonly known as mortal sin. They could stand at the altar table, and, by the grace of God, call the Only-begotten Son into their anointed hands to be shared with the hungry ones outside the altar rail.

As a prelate, the Cardinal recalled his dreams of youth adventurous when he said: "The trails blazed by the heroic Catholic missionaries through forests, atop mountains, across rivers, and over prairies have developed into triumphal highways along which the Catholic faith has erected hundreds and hundreds of temples and tabernacles to our Eucharistic King." As the expanding panorama of world history with its drama and leading players opened up to his eyes, the figure of Christ grew ever more majestic. He saw world conquerors on their knees before the Man God, even as the adventurous and learned Magi had bowed in adoration before the Babe enthroned upon Mary's bosom in the scene of the Epiphany. He saw his divine Hero in his fearless demonstrations of chivalrous love for His

Mother and Queen all through the days of His hidden and public life. He may have wished that he had been left his mother for emulation, but he found a satisfying opportunity to evince his heart's chivalry through fearless display of love for his aunt, his Mother Church, and his Mother Mary.

Christ, the Hero of his youth, was growing daily in his heart as he contemplated the Master's popularity with the Jewish masses who hung upon His message for the three days of His Sermon on the Mount. He saw his divine Hero's fellow men aroused to jealousy over His success, and a resentment of what they considered an invasion of their monopolized province. They saw their own downfall in His promise to establish His Father's Kingdom on earth to complete the old, and merely introductory order, of divine reign.

It was clear to Patrick Hayes that Christ's appeal to His youthful disciples, and His defense of them against the rigorists among the Pharisees who objected to their plucking corn on the Sabbath, had an appeal to the youths of all ages, even his own. Christ was constantly growing in his eyes as the divine Exponent of love for youth, absolutely natural, as the necessary basis of graces emanating from supernatural sources. The young God Man's chivalrous love for His Mother and Queen was studied and imitated closely by the young man during his high school and college days.

Brother Edmund, who had taught Patrick

Hayes in De La Salle Institute, said afterward of his one-time pupil: "It required no prophetic vision to see in Patrick Hayes' boyhood the gradual ascent that was to take place in his life. He studied for the sake of study; he disliked honors, and was devoted to the idea of a career in the Church."

An incident of Archbishop Hayes' boyhood, mentioned by His Eminence in an address delivered to the Catholic Club of New York at the reception given on the evening of the day when he was invested with the Pallium, he told in the following words: "I was at old De La Salle Institute at the time, and George Lavelle, who was also at De La Salle, gave me a ticket for the installation of Archbishop Corrigan at St. Patrick's Cathedral. I went to the Cathedral, and, American boylike, I kept going forward until I found myself just behind the throne. I was ambitious, it seems, even then, because I remember climbing up a little on the pillar behind the throne, so anxious was I to get a view of the Archbishop; and it was a glory to me to have the privilege of getting so close to the Archiepiscopal throne. I don't know whether the spirit entered into me then, and helped me along the road, but I feel I ought to thank George Lavelle for giving me that ticket to the Cathedral!"

The absence of his own mother in the flesh prompted him to a deeper devotion to the Mother of Mankind. In a Christmas pastoral, 1921, Archbishop Hayes gave expression to his heart's youthful fealty to Mary, writing to his people: "The Virgin Mother of God is placed before all womanhood as an example of purity, devotion, and duty. Her whole being is consecrated by the exalted office of motherhood. Christ would not only be a Child, but He would have a Mother, and an immaculate one."

As his mind studied the Holy Family, his heart's yearning to be another Christ grew more and more intense. In his chats with us neophytes of the priesthood in Cathedral College, he frequently referred to the joy in the boyish heart of Samuel when he was called to service in the Temple. He, Patrick Hayes, realized the climax of youth's intellectual triumphs as he studied the twelve-year-old Boy in the Temple, holding the savants of the Old Law entranced while He tutored them in truths which threw light, all but dazzling, upon the true story confided to the Jewish people through the prophets and psalmists. Patrick Hayes wondered whether his teachers and parents could be speaking in literal statements when they told him that the priest is another Christ, a man empowered to exercise the prerogatives of God in the spiritual sphere through the administration of the Sacraments.

It was with an hourly whispered "Lord! I am not worthy!" that he began his days of preparation for the eternal priesthood of Christ. In holy diffidence of soul, he learned and repeated hourly the words that were on his shield of office when he passed from Time—"Stay with us, O Lord!" Years later, when he addressed thousands assembled to do honor to the University of San Francisco, a center of learning established in 1880, as St. Ignatius College, he described the great institution of learning as one "enveloped in the aura of erudition that has flowed from the Church throughout the centuries. Here in the harmony and unity of order established by God's law, science and faith, the natural and the supernatural, are properly coordinated . . . Here science is not separated from God, and is permitted to move along in an orbit that recognizes neither origin nor end except it be demonstrated by experimentation . . . St. Ignatius College is in truth a school of Christ!"

In 1932 he issued a Pastoral letter that bespoke the ideals and aspirations of his own youth, the same still fervently aglow within the breast that he gave to Christ to make His tabernacle daily: "It is a school for young men specially selected for qualities of piety, goodness, and holiness; and the need of the protection and training which Cathedral College affords is certainly evident to all, particularly in our time."

He went on to give an unconscious revelation of his own youthful aspirations when he said: "The fastening of vocations to the religious life and to the priesthood is an obligation not only of the priest and the religious, but also of the parent and guardian. The cultivation of the word of God in the hearts of the faithful, through preaching and the

PATRICK HAYES WITH HIS MOTHER

ON BOARD SHIP: JANUARY 12, 1921

ministration of the Sacraments, requires a plenitude of laborers in the ministry."

If there was ever an exponent of self-determination as to the reality of God's inviting one into the service of the King of Kings and the Great High Priest, it was the youth Patrick Hayes. His teachers, even as his relatives at home, abstained rigorously from any word that might move him to cater to their holy wishes rather than to his heart's absolute conviction that the Master of all vocations had chosen him to be one with Him in priestly elevation and administrations. The youth was happily aware of the joy in the hearts of his classmates as they envisioned future achievements in the spheres of business and professional activities. They bragged to him enthusiastically of their future success as barristers, physicians, as men of public office, as masters of art and architecture. For the men into whose keeping were placed the souls of children and youth seeking truth in the halls of education he offered prayers. But he had only prayers to the Giver of all gifts for fortitude and growth in grace to scale the heights of the mountain that pierces the clouds and brings the priest to an elevation above his fellows through God's humility.

It was a happy group of neighbors who gathered with the Egans in their modest apartment after the return from the youth's graduation exercises in Manhattan College. The young man who was the center of the neighborhood's gaze was characteristically embarrassed as they pored over the Kelly Medal for Philosophy and the Devlin Medal for the Classics, which he had received that day. These two discs were to the simple folk of his home area symbols of great intellectual achievement in the halls of learning. To his kin he was the Boy in the Temple, even as he was to the neighbors who went to him for enlightenment on matters of interest in history, geography, mathematics, and Christian Doctrine. But he looked up to them as untutored sources of wisdom achieved only through sincere and uninterrupted application, combined with experience. He was more the child than ever as he realized the greatness of that altruistic element in human society which endures to the end—to the bench in the shop, to the beat on the policeman's post, to the hod of mortar, and to the range in the kitchen, in order that Youth beloved by them can have the joys of higher education which grim necessity denied themselves.

With Christ, his youthful Hero in the Temple, "he went down, and was subject to them."

CHAPTER III

CATHOLIC AND PRIEST

IN following the design in the texture out of which Patrick Joseph Hayes' life and character were woven, we inevitably come to the solidifying element which was the very essence of his whole career. To take his Catholicity for granted without looking at him in the light of Catholicity's earmarks would be like taking the Catholic Church for granted as just another organization, without studying the plan of Christ Who gave His life to found it.

Patrick Cardinal Hayes was a Roman Catholic as all the world knows. His membership in the Church Militant was the rock upon which was built the edifice of his life. Purposeful in all his administrative acts, the great majority of which aided in rounding off the rough edges of men's economic and spiritual needs, he threw his energies into secular affairs as one part of the work being directed from the throne of God.

No fact was so important to him as the fact of Christ's birth, life and Crucifixion; and the Crucifixion implies in one word the Resurrection and the Ascension, for if those had not been consummated the Crucifixion would not have been significant. Christ appeared as man. He was God in the flesh, symbolizing the universality of all things; perpetuating Himself in the institution of the Roman Catholic Church. "When you see Me," He said, "you see God the Father." These few words sum up past, present and future; for when success has been reached, or failure felt, when wars have been won and lost, and captains and kings have departed, God the Father will be waiting for men to come and begin living the eternal present.

For that moment Cardinal Hayes gave over his days and his energies. Ordination to the holy priesthood was the aspiration of his youth. "All power is given to Me in heaven and earth . . . Go ye therefore and teach all nations . . ." Christ chose the Church as medium to exercise His omniscience through the representation of his bishops, one of whom perpetuates the universality of Christ Himself in matters of dogma. The descendants of Peter speak for all time and to all contemporaries. The bishops are the fullness of the priesthood, living the Christ within them.

The Roman Catholic Church is Christ perpetuated. Its perpetuity rests on His immortality. Patrick Cardinal Hayes lived that promise; his life was an edification of his undying belief and faith in the Catholicism he gave himself to. His own words are as invulnerable as the Church itself. "Irrespective of patristic testimony, whether interpreted one way or another, the stubborn fact of history is that Peter lives on, as Christ promised—the Rock on which the Church was built to endure until the end of time. The Rock, Peter, immovable and impregnable, has resisted, throughout the Christian era, the corrosion and disintegration of time, heresy, schism, human passion, tyranny of princes, not to speak of calumny of a diabolical character. Christ's promise, however, has not failed: the gates of hell shall not prevail against His Church."

His mirroring of the Divine Benefactor extended to an uncommon love for children. He spent long hours during the year, never omitting Christmas Day, among the little ones in the foundling homes where he talked playfully with the waifs whom Pleasure could not tolerate. But he proved what genuine pleasure it was to re-enact scenes from our Lord's life. "Suffer little children to come unto Me." Cardinal Hayes, a child in all his years, could not have proved his Catholicity had he not yearned and striven to emulate the sweetness of a child. How well he succeeded in his emulation he was too humble ever to admit.

His prelate's insignia was his constant prayer: *Mane Nobiscum Domine!* Stay with us, O Lord! And in his plea is heard the confidence of the man in his Hero. His Hero cannot fail. "Just as the Christian calendar began with the Birth of Christ the Savior, so also will the Christian era end with the final glory of Christ the Judge, Who will come to measure all men, all nations and all events according to the standards of Mount Sinai, Bethlehem,

the Mount of the Beatitudes, the Garden of Gethsemane, and Mount Calvary."

"I am with you all days, even to the consum-
mation of the world" kept ringing in his ears like
a victory song; or better, like a priest's absolution in
the ears of a shriven sinner. It was a promise fulfilled.

His fides is summed up in his words: "Innocence of children, purity of woman, chastity of
man, poverty, honest toil, humble station, obedience, and patience were embraced, sanctified, and
taught by God Himself as previous and essential for
our welfare here and hereafter. Riches, worldly
honor, exalted position, great learning, and success
—laudable though they be when sought, reached,
and used within right reason—all are secondary, un-
necessary, and often dangerous in God's plan, for
the following of Christ and the salvation of our immortal souls."

At the International Eucharistic Congress held
at Chicago, he gave voice to the Catholic sense of
unity in the Church here and the army of the
Church Triumphant in heaven: "These unite with
us, or rather, we unite with them, in the unbroken
continuity, the doctrinal integrity, and the organic
unity of the promise and the revelation of Christ, the
Lamb of God, Priest and Victim, made manifest in
type and prophecy during the Old Testament, and
in reality and the fulness of truth in the New Dis-
pensation. Our solemn procession today continues

and extends the long line of believers and adorers, going back to the father of the race."

His Holiness Pope Pius XI sent a personal letter to Cardinal Hayes on the occasion of the closing of the Eucharistic Congress. His Eminence had been the Holy Father's Cardinal-Legate at the Congress. The Pope, touched by the report he received of the external manifestation of Catholic faith made by the throngs at Chicago, wrote: "Such a demonstration by the great metropolis of the Western World on the above-mentioned occasion, participated in by the civil authorities, is at the same time solemn witness before the entire world of the deep veneration accorded by your great nation to the Head of the Catholic Church, and has been a source of supreme satisfaction in that it manifests how profoundly rooted in American hearts is that religious spirit which is the source and guarantee of national greatness and prosperity."

Here was America in the eyes of the Pope. It was an appreciation of American democracy, the democracy of Christ revealed to millions in a democracy carved out of Christlike principles. The Pope did more than merely cast his mental vision over the broad Atlantic. He looked and saw sainthood on these shores. During his pontifical reign the first North American martyrs had been canonized. To Pope Pius XI the church in North America owes the honor and the glory of the canonization of our first Saints, the Jesuit Martyrs.

By nature Cardinal Hayes was a man who saw the nations of the universe as one family. His breadth of vision recognized all nations as more than individual groups. Racial politics are dark shrouds cast over men by the limits of their own human weakness. They cut up territory and erect barriers for national and economic "exigencies," which at best are never more than ephemeral. The Cardinal's vision was far more searching. It found the Sons of God, six hundred and ninety millions of them scattered from cottage to palace, from penthouse to tenement, from tent to yacht, from desert to jungle— and still he saw them all children waiting to sit at the feet of their common Father. They were one.

It made him sad to see them war on one another; to adopt a stand-offish air. He himself was the same before foundling, beggar, mayor, prince or scholar: ever at ease. There radiated from him the joy of boyhood which never left him from the early days in the old Five Points of New York, when he scurried through the snow to serve Mass or join his fellows in a game. Why a few earthly years, be they ever so graying to the hair or creasing to the skin, should move men to don garbs that would seem to make one better than another, he could not understand. Dignity meant, essentially, gentleness, and gentleness could mean only gentlemanliness to him.

His qualities were an endowment of God and he pitied the man who refused the gifts of God: ". . . a poor creature flinging himself at the door of the world's dark, hopeless tomb, crying like a child in the night, calling for the truth that shall free him from the tyranny of self, for the light of truth, the life of truth, and the law of truth; for Christ, the living, the enlightening, the eternal truth of the ages." To him the worst affliction was the lack of proper citizenship in the eternal democracy of heaven. Without this a man is in despair. Especially do the Cardinal's words refer to those poor sincere ones who somehow or other allow themselvs to remain outside the soul of the Church. Catholicity's contribution to posterity, he said, is democracy. The mark of the genuine aristocrat is the outward gentleness which comes from inward dignity. Cardinal Hayes defined it: "This sublime idealism of peace, justice, order, and happiness is presented through Christ the King to the great and the humble, the learned and the unschooled, the rich and the poor, the liberal and the conservative, yea, even the radical, over all of whom He has the inalienable right to rule." He showed his Catholicity in applying these principles of Christ. It was in fact applied Christian Doctrine.

He was another Christ with love for all, a love which prompted the establishment of Catholic Charities.

Roman Catholics are taught that God became Man in order to reveal to humanity the ideal life as the Supreme Being lived it in His thirty-three years of residence as a Figure of history in Time. In order that man in need might find the God Man accessible with His graces all days and in all places, He multiplied Himself in His representatives empowered to act for Himself, with power of attorney, in the dispensing of His endowment of graces to the needy.

It can be readily understood, then, that an office so intimately associated with the Person of Christ as that of a priest must be handed on with the discernment of selection to be found in God alone. Christ said to His disciples: "You have not chosen Me! I have chosen you!" It is to be inferred that their endowment of free will made them capable of refusing the call to function in life as another Christ, but no creature has the prerogative of choosing the role, except as a response in the affirmative to the invitation of his Principal.

But let us inquire into the process of routine which the young man follows who feels that he must respond to the promptings of conscience and find out for himself whether or not he has a personal call to serve in the priesthood of Jesus Christ. Patrick Joseph Hayes provides us with an exemplary case.

There was in his heart, from childhood's earliest consciousness to his last day, a desire to be ever more intimate with, and nearer to, the Man Who more than nineteen hundred years before said He was in heaven, even here on earth, when He was in the midst of a group of romping children. Patrick

Joseph was told that the same one and only God dwelt in the parish church a few blocks away, and that he still lived on earth, under the form and appearance of Bread, in order that He might find a place within the breasts of children and their like in purity. He firmly believed that the God Who knows all things was happy to dwell close to his own heart, and to tell him the secrets of a happy life here. He whispered his problems to the divine Friend within his bosom, and found the light that made his studies easier. He found his God and Friend encouraging him to enjoy himself playing games, even as He had told the children of His own days on earth. The only fear he harbored was that of driving his constant Companion away by committing a sin. The folks at home—his father, his uncle, and his aunt—were one with the parish priest and his consecrated or lay teachers in school in telling him that the best kind of good time was to be found in having Christ, the God Man, as his Protector and Playmate. Laughter was placed before him as the hymn his divine Friend loved to hear. The Sisters in their instructions taught him the story of Christ by explaining the Rosary to him. It was to him the biography of Mary and her divine Son, a ready reference and chronicle for him when he would know the Sacred Heart of his Hero and his Hero's Queen.

The more intimately Patrick Hayes studied the humanity of his Lord, the more palpable became the divinity radiated by the Sacred Heart. His studies in logic were a source of ever-deepening conviction that his divine Master would be more of a mystery to the human intellect were He possessed of but human nature alone. His admission of His divinity clarified the mystery of His towering magnitude above all history's greatest. In philosophy he studied the several systems for comparison and found the Son of Man unique in doctrine emanating from the omniscient mind. The thoroughly ordered sequence and development of his studies in theology, dogmatic and moral, were a fascinationg confirmation of the truths he found in his courses in Scripture.

His reverence and love for Christ as Eternal Mystery incarnate were given expression in his words uttered later in life in paying tribute to his divine Hero. "It is He Whose majestic stature, divine teaching, and inspiring example live on through all the centuries that are and that ever can be. He is the way, the truth, and the life, that mark and bless with surety, safety, and happiness, the pathways of human progress, both in time and in eternity." He studied the majesty in Christ and found that it was, is, and will ever be a synonym for divine simplicity reflected in all humanity's great. His words illumine his concept of priesthood: "Lest the glory of the divinity and the majesty of kingship awe and terrify the children of men, Christ, through the wisdom of the Father, presents Himself as the Shepherd King. He would rule the mind and heart of man with all simplicity, kindliness, humility, and self-sacrifice of a shepherd. No room in His sacred Heart for lust of power, tyranny of injustice, avarice of riches that have all too regularly marked the rule of earthly princes!" It was this, his concept of Christ, as vivid in the postulant for Holy Orders as in the Prince of the Church, that caused him to wonder at the daring of the Church Fathers to designate priests as "other Christs." He found that the ego in each aspirant must be dissolved utterly to make way for the indwelling of Christ, the supreme Master, in the soul of His disciple or ambassador.

He found his divine Hero, Christ, more accessible through routine study of the Church Fathers. Their unanimous verdict of divinity, revealed in His utter simplicity, made the study of these master intellects a daily delight. "No visionary of the most idealistic Utopian philosophy," he said, "for the betterment and elevation of humankind could dream of, imagine, or conceive a state of perfection comparable to the power, the dignity, the happiness, and the destiny with which the Holy Eucharist blesses our weak and lowly nature." It was this concept of Christ, growing daily in the youth studying the history of mankind, which fascinated and humiliated the aspirant who was told that he was called to be "another Christ." His unalterable faith in the grace of God's power to elevate the human soul called to serve as an instrumentality in the hands of the Omnipotence was all that sustained him in his resolve to lay all at the feet of the Master, for Him to mold the clay of which he was formed, and to breathe into it His own image as the High Priest eternal.

There are few of us who do not cherish as holy memories the nights before Christmas when, as children, we retired early to feign sleep and to await the advent of the ruddy-faced, bearded, jolly invader of the family premises who was going to leave before the fireplace the treasures for which we prayed nightly in Advent. Patrick Joseph Hayes was in a kindred elation of soul as he luxuriated in anticipation of the supreme moment of Time and Eternity for him. Often in chats with me he gave utterance to the most sacred of all his recollections, those that went back to the twenty-four hours of his Ordination day. When he first heard his teacher state the truth that the Roman Catholic priest is another Christ, he accepted the phrase as a justified, rhetorical exaggeration. As years of study and meditation progressed in the seminary, the reality of the words became daily more startling. He often thought of the pitiful greeting that would be given the man who stated that he would one day be another Michelangelo, another Washington or Lincoln. But now he found himself accepting as literally applied to himself the overwhelming designation, "another Christ." He was somewhat encouraged by recalling the words of St. Paul, "I live now; yet not I, but Christ liveth in me!" The saving words "not I" helped him to understand at least a little better the possibility of accepting the title. The entrance of Christ into the soul of one of His creatures to take possession of it necessitated the deletion of the self to make way for the dwelling therein of the Creator and Master Who would use him as a human instrumentality to do the works of God among His creatures. The divine Hero of his boyhood was about to endow His disciple with the exercise of divine prerogatives in His holy Name. As Peter had said to the stricken man, "In the name of Jesus Christ, arise and walk!" so would he be permitted to speak to those stricken along life's roadside by the malady of sin, and to those eternally dead, victims of the same disease, and to give them through the Sacramental graces of Penance the power to rise into the freshness of childhood's unsullied vitality before the Judge of the living and the dead.

He mused upon the anticipated thrills of standing by the bedsides of the faithful, awaiting the coming of the last respiration in the sphere of Time, often restored to physical as well as to spiritual soundness by the graces received with Extreme Unction. He visualized with hope and fear the overwhelming moment when it would be his privilege to call to the altar, into his own anointed fingers—yes, into his own very breast—the Son of God Who would be as real a Presence within his bosom as He was in the Cenacle on Holy Thursday night of the first Holy Week. All through his being there echoed the

"Domine! non sum dignus!" of the ruler spoken more than nineteen hundred years before. The very thought of his being endowed with the priestly power to give existence in Time to the Christ of Ascension Thursday was to him a truth as appalling in its suggestion of personal responsibility, as it was desirable beyond the dreams of prophets and kings. The latter would consider the very aspiration a sacrilege were it not prompted by the God Whose humility established the truth for the perpetuation of Himself, in His chosen other selves, until the end of Time.

The retreat of the deacon, Patrick Joseph Hayes, in preparation for his Ordination had been made in characteristic serenity of manner, but the heart within him was burning with eagerness for the great moment, when the Holy Spirit would descend into his heart to impress upon it the image of another Christ. In his latter days, addressing the members of the Catholic Actors' Guild, he revealed to his hearers a suggestion of his heart's thrill in being called to fill the role of Christ in the Galilee to which he was assigned by his ecclesiastical superiors. "To every man and woman is appointed a part in the unfolding of the sublime drama of human existence. Every Christian man and woman should take it upon himself or herself to point the way to regeneration, which is only to be found in a beautiful faith in God . . . To the worldly votary, the Little Poor Man of Assisi is not the great and ardent lover of Christ Crucified, nor the seraphic imitator of Christ's virtues and life. Francis is rather pictured as a charming child of nature, a romantic and poetic troubadour of the sun and the stars, the flowers, the woods, and the birds and the fishes; an outstanding herald of a new era of social reform. Some there are who do not hesitate to so misunderstand this true follower of Christ as to see in him a new patron of a creedless cult and a carefree philosophy of life . . . Saint Francis, marvellously endowed with rare gifts of nature and grace, who 'sparkled like a star shining in the depth of night and like the dawn dispersing the darkness,' can be justly interpreted only in the shadow and light of Christ Crucified. The imprint of the wounded and lanced Body of the Redeemer upon the very flesh of Francis opens to the world the vista of the heights and depth of the supernatural faith, the flaming ardor that overwhelmed the soul of this extraordinary lover of the Cross . . . After seven hundred years his exalted and ecstatic spirituality does not deter, but urges the most unpretentious of the children of men to practical sanctity through humility, charity, self-denial, contempt of honors and riches, childlike simplicity and obedience—to those virtues of the Christian life which are the very foundation and test of all true and abiding holiness."

In such words the man ordained to serve as the priest gave utterance to his dreams when he was a student for the priesthood. To be another Christ

was indeed to him a daring aspiration to a title that
would appal the stoutest heart, were it not sanc-
tioned by the saints called to immortal glory. But
the awed soul of the youth was nonetheless buoyant
and rejoicing. The dream of the boy who was told
that he could, by the grace of God, be his own divine
Hero, and exercise His delegated powers, was about
to come true for the man awaiting the consecrating
words of Ordination! He dwelt upon Christ as the
divine and inexhaustible Source of temporal as well
as of eternal joy. He saw Him with the youth of His
day, with His disciples whose hearts He filled with
the happiness that is theirs who linger in love about
the one Hero they can literally worship. He saw the
youthful Christ as their divine Master, and at the
same time a Man who catered to their desire for
feasting and levity. He saw Him as the Figure so
popular with His contemporaries in Judea that they
basked in the sunshine of His personality while He
taught the doctrine of peace on earth. He saw Him
as the Figure so popular with the people of His
day and nation that the worried and jealous Pharisees would remove Him forever from the arena they
dominated. "Your association with Christ," he said
in an address to his priests in later years, "can mean
nothing unless you keep in your hearts the nearness
to Christ which is your sacred heritage. The modern
world, for all its mechanical progress, for all its in
many ways artificial progress, is uncertain of its destiny, and is not counting the cost of its advancement,

which is largely physical and not spiritual." Such thoughts as these had thrilled the mind of the candidate for Holy Orders on the eve of acceptance by his divine Master. He was about to receive the divine powers which would give him the dignity of walking the ways of men as another Christ! Only God could conceive of a gift, born of divine humility, so overwhelming in its personal significance to the humble recipient!

It was in the exercise and application of Christ's powers within himself that he found a full realization of life. His first Mass was a drama in which he found himself the embarrassed hero, as he spoke his lines and trod in the footsteps of the Christ of the Cenacle, and of Calvary's elevation. "The divine plan was to put man into the world to master the world. Hence the need of great fidelity to practical devotion, especially to every form of homage to the Divine Presence on the altar. Here we really and truly 'often sit down with Christ.' " His was the thrill, known to him for the first time on his Ordination Day, of calling to himself and the people the God Who "put man into the world to master creation." The same great God was the Servant of His priest, readily responding to the sacerdotal call summoning the Real Presence into his own unworthy presence! We neophytes who sat under him in Cathedral College learned something of his concept of the joy that is the priest's who lives with Christ hourly, "sitting down with Christ," at ease in the comfort of a son who knows when consorting with his devoted father and mother that he is welcome. To the graduates he said then, as later to other graduates: "May we ask you in this year of graduation, and the years which will follow, to go out as apostles and ministers of the Eucharist, and by your lives and examples show your faith and your deep love, your yearning desire to have others love and serve Christ likewise?"

The joy of living in Time as another Christ was again given beautiful expression in an address to his priests on retreat. "The most stupendous and the most awe-inspiring facts of humankind are the Creation, the Incarnation, and the Redemption. Through contemplation of these historic events in the mystic drama of the Mass opens up the supreme university of thought, research, and study of the un-created as well as the created, the spiritual as well as the material, the supernatural as well as the natu-ral." He found a holy consolation, that was a source of joy as well as of pity, as he exercised the priestly privilege of sacramental absolution for those who were eternally dead through lapses into mortal sin. He blushed with a sense of unworthiness every time he spoke for Christ the words that summoned the dead penitent from the tomb into life eternal, again accessible through the grace of God released in the Sacrament of Penance. Visits to the bedsides of the dying, where he was empowered to bedeck them in the wedding garment to be worn, of necessity, by

all attending the King's banquet, were recurring epi-
sodes of sacred drama that prompted him to meditate with increasing humility upon the confidence
placed by God in men called to act for Him in dispensing heaven's wealth. The more vivid became
the realization of his call to act as another Christ,
the more intense became his prayer that the self
might be dissolved in order that Christ might use
him as His instrumentality to dispense redemption's
graces to those in need.

The scene of his Ordination into the Roman
Catholic priesthood on the birthday of his Blessed
Mother Mary, September 8, 1892, was to him the
most lustrous event of his life. This day was to him
one of the greatest of all holy days in the Christian
calendar. He dwelt in thought upon the celebra-
tions of lay groups expressing their joy in the birth
of the great national figure, George Washington. He
joined with his fellow countrymen in tributes to
Abraham Lincoln expressed on his returning natal
days. But his heart pondered with awe the relatively
greater significance, ever growing more personal, of
the birthday of the woman who shared her beauty
of body and soul with the God of history's immortals. He dwelt upon the singular honor paid her by
immortality's divine King in placing her in the
realm of Time to help undo the evil effects of Eve's
lapse in Eden's garden. He mused upon the honor
done all womanhood by the Father's selection of a
Maiden to give birth to the second Adam, the God

Man, who could neither deceive nor be deceived. Voicing his reverence for Christian womanhood, lay and religious, he offered his thanks to "our Heavenly Father for the valiant women we all know—and their name is legion—who with the highest ideals of wifehood and motherhood carry on heroically the honor of the family. Neither height nor depth, nor sorrow nor pain, nor sin of husband, nor ingratitude of children, nor privation, nor loss, nor opportunity of comfort, nor lure of pleasure, can tempt such noble women to shirk their duty or break up their home. Silently, patiently, cheerfully, and holily they spend themselves and are spent for the spiritual and temporal welfare of their own flesh and blood in their children."

He dared to see himself as the priest called to fill the role of Mary as he called from heaven, with the words of Consecration at the Mass, the Babe Who dwells among men as the Source of temporal and eternal joy for those given personal possession of Him at the altar rail. As a loyal son of Mary, there throbbed in his soul a joy echoing hers in the Annunciation as she heard the Archangel Gabriel's words, "Hail! full of grace! The Lord is with thee, and blessed is the fruit of thy womb!" Even as the Holy Spirit had come upon her, so did the Third Person take residence in him through the sacramental grace of Ordination. "Christ alone can call the simple shepherd from the hills, the humble ploughman from the field, the unlettered fisherman from the nets, the honest toiler from the shop, the money-changer from the bench, the beggar from the roadside, the leper from the lazaretto, the woman of shame from the haunts of vice, even the thief from the gibbet, to come and sit down with kings and princes, the learned and the great, around his Eucharistic table, to break and partake of the Bread of Angels, His Own Body and Blood." These words, expressed later in life, are the outpourings of a priestly soul conscious of Ordination's joys. It may not be amiss to recall his words on the overwhelming import of the Eucharistic rite: "No priest nor Pope, no King nor Cardinal can entertain you at any such banquet table as does the Master Himself, Who gave you His infinite love and power which are in His Sacred Heart. He felt nothing but love Himself, and He gave you the means of purity!"

The crowning charm of Patrick Joseph Hayes was his simplicity of heart and naturalness of manner. The mystic who had, a few minutes before, scaled the skies and buried himself in the Sacred Heart of his God, could lapse without effort into the laughter of ingenuous boyhood as he mingled with the passersby in conversation on current doings in the world. He never encouraged the dour, drab, or self-repressive philosophy in his spiritual subjects. "The children of the bridegroom rejoice when he is with them" was his constant recollection of his divine Master's counsel to the self-scandalized Pharisees. He saw the devotional in spiritual expression of faith as a challenge to men and women all too subservient to the demands of current dictators of fashions in expressing their misconceptions of personal independence in religion's conventional observances. He was ever himself, and that self was given in its entirety to Christ, the ever-present Lord ruling his heart and mind in a regime of sustained joy. "Stay with us, O Lord!" was imprinted upon his Ordination card and upon his heart's eternal recesses.

CHAPTER IV

The Charitable Executive

THE archdiocese of New York is not a corporation in itself. Every unit of Catholic activity within its confines is a separate corporation which freely chooses the Ordinary ruling over his assigned territory as its president. The various institutions dedicated to activities charitable and educational are separate corporations that invite the reigning prelate to serve as the president of each, and elect him as such when he consents. As the head of the Archdiocese, he is assisted by a Board of Consultors who are called to be his advisors in the solution of current problems. They are happy to serve their ecclesiastical principal without being invested with any legal status, civil or canonical, and without any control through voting.

The Father Hayes who was assigned to act as an assistant in the parish of Auxiliary Bishop Farley was soon found to be a young priest of methodical life, of quiet initiative, and of native readiness to respond to the suggestions of his superior's calls for personal assistance. After a period of test as secretary to Archbishop Farley, his talents for orderliness and organization were demanded for bigger responsibilities. Each diocese transacts its official business from its Chancery Office, the director of which is the Chancellor. He is the ecclesiastical notary of the diocese and draws up all written documents involved in official transactions necessary in its government. He cares for, arranges, and indexes these documents in the diocesan archives, which are depositories for records of dispensations, Church trials, and similar papers of official import.

The charm of the ecclesiastical official, assigned to carry out the routine of daily transactions involved in archdiocesan business, had its appeal to all who were brought into touch with Patrick Joseph Hayes. He was ever the same soft-spoken, smiling host, who dispelled timidity in the average postulant for enlightenment and for help in meeting personal, if not intimate difficulties. There was no suggestion of the hurried or distraught in his manner of transacting official business. There was nothing of the aloof specialist, probing the masked features of a patient troubled with invisible irregularities. There was nothing of the staged abruptness that would convey to those impressed by mannerisms, the idea of his every passing second's being an important milestone lost to progress on the highway of Time. He was simply his own, easy, natural self as he went about his Father's business.

Msgr. J. Francis A. McIntyre has given me an appreciation of his predecessor in the office of Chancellor in which he remarks: "I feel it is quite true that the Cardinal, in his judgments, was palpably guided by the Holy Spirit. It was quite remarkable and frequently observed that when a report was presented to His Eminence, with a recommendation that was expected to be acceptable, he would look over the plan submitted, and, in a casual way, suggest a different solution. That solution would be so sound and feasible that immediately the proposer recognized it as the real solution.

"In financial affairs His Eminence exercised a very long-headed viewpoint. He had keen appreciation of the value of that indefinable, subtle, and elusive thing called credit. His judgments were not made on the effects of the moment, but on the outcome to the Church for a long period of time and in other parts of the country. In other words, he applied in his dealing in material things the spiritual principle that the Church is alive eternally, whereas material-minded considerations are purely temporal. His judgments never wavered because of a momentary or temporary advantage, but he viewed always the picture presented to him in the light of the interest of all concerned, with the result that his decision was eminently fair and considerate. Furthermore, behind his business dealings was always a generous and strong confidence in the honesty and integrity of his fellow man. He treated others with justice, consideration, and charity, and expected that they, in turn, would treat them likewise. He would graciously comment that he had not been disappointed."

The caller who came for advice in Canon Law and its application to individual problems was greeted by a pleasant host who so ordered the expenditure of his time and energy as to permit him to plan, without serving two masters, the establishment of an institution that was his dominant aspiration from the earliest days of his priesthood. He studied the local scene in the Archdiocese, and came to the conclusion that it would be to the greater glory of God if there were established an educational unit specializing in the training of youth praying for a place in Christ's priesthood. His abilities as an executive prompted him to meditate upon the benefits that would multiply if young men who nurtured a common spiritual ideal were brought together in daily association. He envisioned an archdiocesan preparatory seminary as an institution that would not only serve to foster early vocation to the priesthood, but would likewise serve to assist youth in doubt as to the reality, or otherwise, of a call from the Heart of Christ to His chosen disciples to prepare for the eminence of service.

In spite of the many demands of the Chancery, and of obligations in personal service to Archbishop Farley, he found the energy, wit and time to plan and to realize the establishment of Cathedral College in 1903. It was he who arranged to house its activities in the building which stands on Madison Avenue, New York, and extends the length of the block from Fifty-first to Fifty-second Street. He mobilized the priests and laymen necessary to meet the curriculum's demands in teaching staff. He arranged for the maintenance that called for resources apt to frighten the less stalwart in soul. And as its first president he personally supervised the many departments and operations of an educational institution recognized by the State Regents as a college duly established.

Dr. James J. Walsh said: "In the meantime honors from Rome began to come to him. In 1903, the year of his appointment as Chancellor of the Archdiocese and of his organization of Cathedral College, he received his first official recognition from Rome in the form of the degree of Doctor of Divinity. Four years later, in 1907, Rev. Dr. Hayes was appointed domestic prelate by His Holiness Pope Pius X with the title of Monsignor. Seven years later Monsignor Hayes while in Rome with Cardinal Farley was appointed Auxiliary Bishop of New York on June 1, 1914, by Pope Pius X whose death as the result of the shock of the awful war that had broken out was to come only a few months later. Each of these positions imposed new and special duties and Dr. Hayes proved not only equal to them but demonstrated a power of control over details which showed very clearly his own strength of personality and his ability to understand men and see the deeper meaning of questions behind details that came to him. In the midst of all he won and held the friendship, cordial and enduring, of all those with whom he was brought into contact and especially in whose regard he had to fulfill the duties of the various offices which he held.

"As Chancellor of the Archdiocese of New York Monsignor Hayes had to keep in touch with not only every church but every clergyman in the diocese. There were many hundreds of churches and still more hundreds of clergymen, but so thoroughly did he accomplish this work which came to him that it was often said that he knew all the priests in the diocese, not only by name, but in the intimate personal way that enabled him to understand their problems sometimes almost better than they did themselves. He knew their histories, knew what they were doing for their parishes and what they were planning to do, was well aware how they were fulfilling their priestly duties and recognized the zeal they had for the Church. If these duties as chancellor were all he had to do, perhaps the task would not have seemed so great. But he was, besides, the secretary of the Archbishop and the president of Cathedral College and these duties added detail upon detail of responsibility that must have occupied every moment of the day and might very well be expected at times to invade some of the night.

"Even all this however does not complete the tale of his duties. He was a contributor of important articles to the Catholic Encyclopedia as well as to the Catholic University Bulletin. He wrote for the *North American Review* an interpretation of the new marriage law, *Ne temere* (so called because of the initial Latin words in the papal decree promulgating it) , which was an admirable piece of work for its clearness, accuracy and brevity. Such an article was needed very much at that time because there had been rather serious misunderstandings with regard to the new Roman Catholic marriage law. It had been said, though of course quite without reason, that the Church absolutely refused to recognize the validity of marriages contracted without the Church's blessing. This was not true except for members of the Church thoroughly aware of the Church's legislation in the matter. This legislation was for Catholics and not for those outside of the Church. The Sacrament of Marriage has for its ministers the wedded couple themselves and not the clergyman who performs the ceremony. Monsignor Hayes brought out very well the distinctions in this matter and made it very clear just what the Church legislation aimed at accomplishing in order to make matrimony more sacred and solemn than the tendency of the modern world was prone to permit it to be."

When the aging Archbishop of New York, John M. Farley, found the duties of the office a burden to be shared with a younger man, it was natural that he should turn to one who had been for years his loyal assistant in carrying out the duties of his episcopal office. But the older man had only the privilege of intimating his preference, based upon his knowledge of talents applied with zeal to duties assigned in lesser offices held by Monsignor Patrick Joseph Hayes. The set procedure for the nomination of bishops in the Roman Catholic Church calls for those in the episcopacy to send every two years to their metropolitans a list of priests regarded as worthy of episcopal rank. The metropolitan presents these names to the Apostolic Delegate who forwards them to the Roman Congregation of the Consistory, where they are recorded for the Holy Father's reference in selecting bishops for vacancies, or for newly created sees.

A Bishop-Auxiliary is called to assist his spiritual chief in the visitations of the parochial units in the diocese, and also in such works as are only within the spiritual power of those enjoying the fullness of priesthood. Confirmation of those called to receive the Holy Ghost and the divine gifts that fortify militants of Christ to meet and conquer the forces of the world, the flesh, and the devil, is a Sacrament which can be administered only by one of episcopal powers. So likewise the Ordination of worthy postulants to the dignity of other Christs is a spiritual power given by the Holy Spirit to bishops alone.

Monsignor Hayes was elevated to the episcopacy in 1914 by Pope Pius X. He was installed as pastor of St. Stephen's Church, New York City, and carried on the duties of a shepherd responsible for his parochial flock. His work was made a joy through the co-operation of his assistants in the parish, who

found living with him a sustained period of contentment and inspiration to increasing zeal. The rectory
was blessed, through his paternal sympathy and ever-
ready hospitality, with the happiness of the Holy
Family in Nazareth. All were one with him in devotion to the divine Guest of Honor residing in the
tabernacle of the church next door. It was here, as
in his other spheres of executive action, that he was
the simple priest co-operating happily with his fellows of the cloth. There was no suggestion in his
manner or speech of the absorbed, brooding, knit-
browed official who is often an exponent of imitated,
rather than true greatness. He was never too busy
in his hours of executive action to pass a pleasantry
with his client or to exchange a wholesome, mirth-
provoking story.

It was his own evident desire to participate in
patriotic service, when the World War broke out in
1914, that resulted in his being selected to organize
and administer the military diocese established by
the Holy Father, Pope Pius X, in the United States
of America. Added to the duties of this office, were
those undertaken by him at the request of the national body of Catholic men enrolled as Knights of
Columbus with Cardinal Farley's warm approval.
He was a director of a drive for funds to be distributed in relieving war's victims, which resulted in a
mass contribution of more than five million dollars.
He was also one of the directing agents in the drive
prosecuted by the United War Works body of altru-

ists, who collected more than one hundred and seventy-five million dollars to be applied in relief to stricken subjects of all creeds.

He was happily and thoroughly equipped by executive endowments and broad experience when he was called to the seat of administration in one of the most sacred of all responsibilities in the world— the Archdiocese of New York. Rev. Martin J. Scott, S.J., says: "What particularly impressed me about Cardinal Hayes was the exquisite balance of his character. Rarely have I known a person in whom were so admirably combined intense religious fervor and strong common sense. Both in public and in private his speech and actions displayed remarkable moderation joined with great firmness of purpose. No wonder he was so universally loved!"

Catholic Charity is Our Lord multiplying the loaves for the five thousand hungry ones who forgot the cares of Time while they listened to the Word made Flesh presenting the beauty of Catholic Charity in the Sermon on the Mount. In more than two hundred agencies in the Archdiocese of New York He is acting today—in hospitals, through the day and the night, to bring healing graces and cheer to the bodies and souls of men and women wasted by fever and pain, or fighting a life and death struggle with cancer, tuberculosis or heart disease.

Cardinal Hayes' concern was not so much with the size and population of his Archdiocese as with the "love and sense of service the people possess." In all the work of the Catholic charitable agencies, he stressed always the importance of *doing*, motivated by sheer personal love for Christ, and love for all who would benefit by the doing. "We must hold and assert all that is effective and wholesome in the work of the past. But we must seek out everything that is helpful in what is new, and effect improvement in the service by adopting the lessons of experience and by improving our standards in the light of newer insight into the social relations of every kind, as these affect the poor."

The words "in the light of newer insight" give the key to Patrick Joseph Hayes' theory of active charity. Modern scientific achievements were to be given practical outlet. But the sick and needy were not to be treated as mechanized instruments at the hands of social science without that same science being deeply concerned with the spiritual phases of these human beings. Therefore, anyone working in social science would be defeating the purpose of social welfare were he or she to mitigate the importance of administering to the spiritual as well as the temporal needs. Workers for charity gain interest on their investment of good works when they consecrate their work to the God of love. It is an investment of capital that wins its dividends in the world of Eternal Love. Noble and inspiring modesty accompanied the organization and continuance of Catholic Charities by Cardinal Hayes, showing the way to all who wanted to participate: "I am taking no glory for myself . . . While it is true that I was the beginner and that perhaps I made it possible for this great work to go on, the carrying on of the Catholic Charities was not due to my individual efforts, nor was it due to the clergy or the splendid Religious; but it was due to the co-operation of the splendid Catholic people who have caught my idea."

Science and the mechanical undertakings of governmental departments for distributing to the indigent must not be taken as anything less than the servants of humanity, he believed and taught. When the agents of charity become condescending towards those they help, then the greatness of the work disappears. Actually, the agents are the servants, and should be grateful for the opportunity to extend openly their love for the creatures of God. "When scientific research, ruling charity out of court, attempts to pry into the origin, the conduct, and the destiny of man, it is doomed from the outset to failure."

The Son of God is the Director of every charitable organization in the world, giving vitality and purpose to his aids, beneficence to the recipients. "With Christ animating organized charity, its spiritual power and its social value are destined to bring down benediction upon the individual and the nation. . . Should it occur that national ideals shift from this base or social values conform to a different standard, Christian charity, which 'never falleth away' can be summoned to serve as the corrective for the one and for the other."

We have come to know that charity means love supreme. Cardinal Hayes saw the Protagonist of Calvary's drama as the Divine Mendicant Who had wept so bitterly for those shortsighted enough to have refused His simple gifts. They had failed to recognize in those gifts the genuine basis, a spiritual sinking fund, of lasting peace and happiness. His Eminence's solicitude for the temporal needs of his charges was an echo of Christ's solicitude for the people of Jerusalem. He dwelt upon the Master overlooking the city, weeping over it, and saying, "If thou also hadst known, and that in this thy day, the things that are to thy peace; but now they are hidden from thine eyes."

"Catholic charity" is another phrase expressing "peace on earth." It is universal benevolence applied habitually to God and neighbor. It is the bond that makes three worlds one under the dominion of Eternal Love. As militants of Christ are His loyalists to death, so suffering souls are His beloved, awaiting entrance into eternal peace with the triumphant, through the charity of man offering prayers and good works to the Divine Mendicant, Who pays their debts to the Father awaiting prodigal sons once afar off but now standing at the open portal of home, beseeching the Host of heaven to tender them the wedding garment of grace.

The Cardinal's diocese, and the world too for

that matter, was seen by this devotee of Christ's charity as the divine Shepherd's own Galilee, multiplied several hundred million times. For the charity of Bethlehem, of Nazareth, of Jerusalem, of Gethsemane, and of Calvary was a charity patterned for a universe which would expand in future centuries, to be peopled by countless millions of men, women and children. The setting of our Lord's life was like a little classroom or lecture hall where great principles were taught to the few who were present; who would go forth to teach all nations whatsoever the Master would have man know.

When His Eminence says, "Our deeds of charity are truly a good investment," we see the Lord of the World as the divine Money-Changer, Who would suffer no intrusion into the Temple of Love on the part of those who had made of it a "den of thieves." Christ changes money into sight for the blind, hearing for the deaf, strength for the halting, and life for the dead through those dedicated to serve Him by ministering to the least. Christ is Catholic Charity in the flesh, and Patrick Joseph Hayes, to whom the imitation of Christ was a code of life, applied himself to shaping his own life after that charitable Flesh. His concept of charity was essentially peace. "When Christian charity departs from the coasts of a nation, peace goes with it." He intended by his words to implant in the children of his ecclesiastical demesne the seeds of tolerance, kindness, and corporal and spiritual mercy. He is called the Cardinal of Charity for reasons far surpassing his construction of human agencies of succor for the needy, the aged, and the crippled. Those agencies in themselves would be no better than the mechanical doling out of meal tickets by any social agency if they were not accompanied by spiritual comforts, emanating from the Sacred Heart of the Benefactor.

The Cardinal saw deeper than the mere financial needs of the poor. Besides the material assistance, there are the rehabilitating sympathies which only personal companionship, understanding, and friendship can give. The unveiling of Christ's heretofore masked beauty on Mount Tabor was His personal act of sharing with us the infinite glory and beauty lying within. On Calvary's mount He proved that His friendship for man extended to every human soul. In the institution of the Holy Eucharist, before He gave His Body in death, He gave to the world not only His Body but also His Soul. Through the Eucharist He enters, Body and Soul, into all men who receive Him, even into the bodies of the least of us. When we are charitable to human beings we are charitable to God, for they are His creatures and in them He lives.

His Eminence founded his concept of charity on this precept. Its scope was not limited to monetary donation, for that, he said, was too easy a way. True charity embraces all our relations with one another, for each of us receives his life and his light from the Divine Giver Who takes up His own life within our beings. "Terrible will be the judgment on us, if, through the failing of our charity, Christ, hidden in His brethren, will receive from the scoffer and the denier of the Cross the welcome and the help refused Him by His adorers!"

His Eminence reminded us of the magnanimity that must be theirs who are privileged to share kinship with the King of Kings, and the Lord of Heaven and earth. He reminded us of the gifts expected of those who would one day enter the Father's House, when he quoted St. John: "Behold what manner of charity the Father hath bestowed on us, that we should be called and should be the sons of God." He suggested the principle of noblesse oblige when he quoted St. Paul to the Ephesians exhorting us to "walk worthy of the vocation in which you are called, with all humility and mildness, with patience, supporting one another in charity." "Our offerings," said the Prince of the Church, "should be as princely as our dignity in the realm of the King of Kings Whose sons we are by adoption."

It was this endowment of Christlike charity in the Cardinal which moved him to bring peace and contentment, through the medium of more than two hundred agencies, into the hearts of his sheep. The latest methods of science and social welfare he employed for the application of charity so that the poor, the sick, and the friendless might have brought into their lives the temporal peace which Christ promised the faithful.

In the Cardinal's mind burned the great motive to serve God by taking care of His "least ones." His motive materialized in the application of the principles of Christ's charity; and his charity was multiplied in every form of human need. "Through the medium of charity," he said, "Christ appears so wonderfully human and man so gloriously divine. The nobility and the value of the human soul shines out never so brightly as in the lights of the love of Christ. . . With Christ animating organized charity, its spiritual power and its social value are destined to bring down benediction upon the individual and the nation."

The present Pontiff, then Papal Secretary to His Holiness Pope Pius XI, of happy memory, in 1931 communicated the following letter to Patrick Cardinal Hayes in tribute for the glorious charitable practices he was so successfully conducting in his See:

"I have the pleasure to inform your Most Reverend Eminence that I have placed in the venerable hands of His Holiness the report of the charitable works of your Archdiocese.

"The august Pontiff was greatly pleased to note that notwithstanding the grave financial crisis afflicting the people of your Diocese, offerings have been given so generously as to surpass your every expectation.

"Beautifully does this demonstrate that the spirit of charity, so widely diffused among the faithful, has made them practice the counsel of the Great Ambrose, who exhorted the Christians of his time: 'Let us have compassion on the infirmities of others; let us help the necessities of others as much as we can, even more than we can.'

"Moreover, the Holy Father is confident that, by the practice of Christian virtues, the causes of the present economic crisis will cease and prosperity will return. From His Heart He imparts the Apostolic Benediction to your Eminence, to the Clergy and the people of your Archdiocese."

The domestic struggle, wherein the industrious are forced to succumb to social adversity through no fault of their own, was of vital concern to Cardinal Hayes. The futile striving against odds insurmountable for the individual facing an international economic depression, he knew only too well, had sooner or later its demoralizing effect on the conscientious heads of families, on youth despairing of its chances to pursue position, and on business men seeking to rehabilitate their organizations. His words, sketching the despondency of a father, reveal his characteristic sympathy and clear-headed understanding of what millions had to face:

"... Downcast and weary he comes back to

them at night reluctant to answer their eager questions. Dollar by dollar he sees his savings slip away. When the lack of proper nourishment and care has undermined vitality, sickness must often be endured without a doctor's care, and the landlord's knock becomes a summons of dread. It is heart-rending for a man to see all that he has fought for and labored for breaking down. With his own health, and that of his dear ones menaced, the home which he had always looked upon as a sanctuary of cheerfulness and love may easily become a place of dissension and discouragement. Yea, more! despairing of relief, he can easily be transformed, under the spell of a fiery demagogue, from a peaceable law-abiding citizen into a dangerous foe of society. Unemployment is a potential social menace of a very radical type."

It was ever the soul's reenforcement which he considered his first duty. The protection of spiritual values, the roots of human society, need charitable offerings to offset the contaminating effects on the soul of a nation which is faced with material desolation.

No system of social order can thrive without the home life of families permeated with the love and devotion which reflect the spirit of generosity and tolerance in Christ's one life. Charity itself penetrates more deeply into the significance of humanity than the publicity attached to huge "drives" often indicates. It is the supreme virtue by which men and women manifest their superiority over animals not blessed by rational faculties. We are rational animals only in word when we allow ourselves to be absorbed in the riotous rush of life, in which individuals pursue life with only the ego and its enrichment as goal. Charity without tolerance is the same as an empty house. It must have warmth, a sympathy for those who find the paths of life barren.

"The sublime presence of Christ," said Cardinal Hayes, "in which Christian charity lives and moves and has its being, imparts to human sympathy and help a heavenly touch and a spiritual power."

It is useless to strive for what men call success if they limit their activity to personal vainglory and material advantage, applying their abilities to the acquisition of property and position as the sole reward of their endeavor. Christian life and Christian success had their embodiment in Cardinal Hayes, who, through his entire life, believed that the greatest and most meritorious success comes from the following of Christ in all our breathing hours. The example of Christ shows us how we are to live, what are to be our aims, and the Cardinal breathed forth the very breath of his Master's simplicity and love far surpassing tolerance. No one was excluded from his kindliness. He once told a friend, "If you ever meet a priest who thinks I have not been kind, I want him to see me and let me be kind."

The wide reputation he gained as the Cardinal of Charity was won by this simple sort of kindness.

The world knew him for his genius in organizing the widespread Catholic Charities in a great city. The relatively few who had regular, intimate contact with him in the affairs of life knew him for a charity which he held out to all, to his domestic staff and to the notables of the world alike. The old saying that a man is never a hero to his valet is not true when applied to His Eminence. He was loved by his domestic retinue, his official assistants, his pastors, and his priests. The millions who mourned him and who had never seem him more closely than from their pews in the Cathedral were inspired by the love which he emptied out of himself and into their souls.

The high purpose of Cardinal Hayes' life—the incessant endeavor to be the Alter Christus—crystalized itself within his being; his body, his thoughts, his soul were placed at the disposal of his divine Master. The impetus behind him was a force having its roots in the Eternal Kingdom of Love, and once he had set himself to be guided toward that Kingdom, he could not have retraced his own steps. The Boy Hero whom he had followed from childhood, grown up with, worked for, received, consecrated bread and wine for, and Whose neglected dependents he had ministered to, was the same Who had died on the Cross with His last words, words of charity for men. This noble life remained the outstanding, unwavering wellspring of knowledge and wisdom, courage and fortitude, which filled him with the grace he needed to live and die the memorable Cardinal of Charity.

His words are clear-cut and impossible of misconstruction by any who read them. They thrill one with desire to serve: "The motive of merely human endeavor does not shine with the glory of Christian charity, seeing that it is prompted by the love of man for man, and merely aims at the human good of man; yet, it is noble, because the line of its activity and the focus of its interests are away from self."

"Away from self" so readily depicts the Cardinal that one is easily tempted to believe that he might have set the phrase up before him to be followed as a daily motto. Away from self into the Heart of the Lord; into the Kingdom of Divine Peace and Compassion.

CHAPTER V

CHRISTIANITY'S DEMOCRAT

THE public is often greatly impressed by what it sees, but too often does not see much further than the outward garb of things or people. It looks at the picture of a king gaudily arrayed in luxurious robes, receiving the homage of cheering admirers. The public thinks, "What a lucky man. Born to riches. Nothing to worry about. Oh, to be king!" Its mind is full of one word, "king," without going into the picture of political conferences, personal jealousies among cabinet members, the masses to be satisfied and the necessity of making judgments which will cause the king to be hated.

We turn the page of a daily paper and there is the picture of a man who has just won a prize for a great painting. We say, "What a lucky man, to win all that money. Everybody will invite him out and toast him." We forget to think back to the painter's hours of drudgery, days of discouragement, his daily need to sustain himself and probably a family. Behind any photograph is a man who has principles, ideals, burdens.

I would like the reader to think of Patrick Cardinal Hayes as something more than just a man in the public eye; more than just a dignitary of the

Church; more than a man who was "lucky" enough to wear red robes and enjoy a position of prestige.

He was also a human being. He rose in the morning and said his prayers, meditated, read his Mass, meditated again in thanksgiving, had his breakfast, and read the morning paper. He took his place in the scheme of life, New York life, American life. In his own estimation Cardinal Hayes was merely another one of the millions who are the ingredients of America. Essentially he thought of himself first as a Catholic, then as Catholic American with duties to perform toward the God of Catholics, first, then toward America. Without his Catholicism his Americanism would have been hollow.

In his own thoughts he was not "exalted." He did not look in his mirror and say to his image, "Just think! I am better than all the other Catholics in the city." He did not say, "How fortunate I am not to be just another poor parish priest slaving away unknown." On the occasion of his sacred elevation to the Cardinalate, however, he *did* say to a large audience, "My thought is one of deepest gratitude for the honors given to one so humble, who would choose rather to serve in the ranks than in a superior position. But God called me, and in response to the command of the Holy Father, I came to receive the high dignity with chastened soul. . . In this moment of joy my soul turns in prayer, gratitude, and affection to the glorious country of which I am proud and happy to be a citizen."

Ecclesiastical honors to him were only the embellishment of his citizenship; his position gave him a greater opportunity to serve his God by serving the sons of God. Always he was a servant of God and man. What an ideal for any president or governor or mayor or employer to follow as the creed of life! Cardinal Hayes' cares were multiplied because in his hands now rested the spiritual destinies of Roman Catholics in the world's metropolis. Americanism he considered a worthless shibboleth if it were not cemented to a foundation which raised to the skies the belief in the King of Kings. "May our nation never forget God!" this shepherd told his flock. "It is our duty as American citizens to give practical profession of our faith in the spiritual dignity of man and in the eternal destiny of the human soul, thereby to assert the sublime elements in citizenship. The Catholic Church is today the religious Faith of twenty million Americans."

In New York City he ruled over his spiritual domain as assigned by the Holy Father of Christendom. A big position to hold and care for without error. Still, New York is only another town in relation to the universe, just as the world's foremost dictators and leaders are merely a few more men, flesh and blood, with the capacity for error and the capacity for salvation, in the mind of God. To regard one's local or worldly position before everything else is foolish. Cardinal Hayes was not a great man because he was the spiritual guide to millions in a small area of America. He was noble because he felt himself a small figure in a representative group whose work comes to fullest materialization in the boundless eternity. Said he, addressing the legislators of Texas, "You know I also am a senator; I am a member of an old, ancient Senate, a Senate that has been at work for a thousand years, a Senate that has driven, that has prayed, that has worked and used its influence toward the civilization of the Christian world. And I am so proud that I sit in the Senate of the Church as a Cardinal, a Senate of seventy members from all parts of the world, and when I sit there as a Cardinal, under my Cardinal's robe is a heart that pulsates with the greatest sentiments of gratitude to the Almighty God that I am at the same time an American citizen. . . ."

Lincoln was his ideal American, the great factor in presenting the Union of States under one flag. Lincoln humbled himself before the King of Kings, asked His guidance, begged His forgiveness. The lanky mid-Western farmer saw all men as brothers, fought to make American men brothers— brothers, because they were the sons of God. Alongside the words of the great liberator are the words of His Eminence: "What America needs is a soul which the Church alone can give. . . No nation, no people, can long endure in peace and safety if racial and religious hatred and class bitterness set at naught Christian brotherhood." Prophetic words which have come to be realized each day in the world's history of the present time.

He saw Lincoln as something more than one more president written up in history texts; something more than a mere contributor to legislation. The Cardinal looked back across the years and saw the wild plains of a vast, untamed land. He saw the sod houses and log cabins of men and women suffering from cold, drought, pain, and exploitation. In his ears he heard the howl of a coyote rising against the wail of wind and storm, and in one of those crude huts he saw a boy stretched on the floor straining his eyes to read a page. The boy Abe was tired from a day's work on the farm; his back had been bent in labor, his skin was dank from sweat. Yet there he was in the half-light of a wood fire, feeding his mind, which ached to find out the rules of logic and justice, the law of God, to be applied in the day's work of being a decent citizen.

Man is the grown product of what the boy, in his diligence or lassitude, has made of himself. Lincoln, the man, had risen from the hard surface before the wood fire to become a decent citizen who led others to be decent citizens. But he rose through the study and inspiration of the Christ ideal. His leadership would have been fruitless had he not made palpable the teachings of his King of Kings.

Prejudice of man against man was a blight on the nation's history in Lincoln's day as it was in the

Cardinal's, a canker that seems to hang on in spite of Christianity. Lincoln recognized and tried to dig it out. Cardinal Hayes recognized it and did everything in his power to erase it. He saw that its roots could not be cut out as a physician cuts out an ordinary tumor with his scalpel. Love of country had to be made love of man for man, not merely a spoken allegiance to a party or flag. The country is more than a map of varicolored states; the love of it must be Christlike, tender, self-sacrificing. "Love of country," he said, "comes with us next to love of God. Speaking as an American, in whom the love of the American flag is almost as sacred as my obligation to Christianity and civilization, I know that the Catholics of this country yield to none of their brothers of any sect in love for the United States." And he continued to define what he meant in a terse sentence: "Love comes from God Who is the Source of all love."

It is obvious from his utterances and actions that Patrick Cardinal Hayes was no mere effigy of a leader. His soul was on fire with the ambition to get men to understand the mystical union existing between the Kingdom of God and the kingdoms of men on earth. The latter belonged to the former, were states in it. He recognized no one race as superior to another, no nationality richer than another, no personal prestige more conducive to sainthood than a lowliness in the democracy of humanity. Everyone was a member of the same great family.

It was the Union of Men for unity with God! Such was the Cardinal's creed of life. Such was his working definition of Catholicism in action toward Americanship and citizenship.

He was a militant patriot. He was the watchman on the tower, ready to single out the enemy and fearless to protect his country and his people from the enemy, whether the foe be rising from within or attacking from without. His leadership, he was aware, required him to be on the *qui vive*. Citizenship meant safeguard of public morals, in the school, home, on newsstands, and in the theatre. It meant, besides, a finger on the pulse of legislation which might affect adversely the economic—and, therefore, the moral—lives of men. He was not one to sit in his house by the side of the road and watch the race of men go by without lending a hand along the way. "The apostles of discontent are growing more numerous. They offer much to our youth, so much as to decide, if possible, even the elections. We must be ever watchful shepherds."

To that end he injected a strong Catholic voice against the welter of obscene magazines that cluttered newsstands; and, with a view to offsetting the free rein of motion picture producers, he was instrumental in forming the National Legion of Decency, which has become the most formidable weapon the Catholic Church in America has ever wielded against purveyors of dangerous forms of entertainment. Birth control he abhorred on more than moral grounds; on practical grounds based, ultimately of course, on morality. It would mean, he foresaw, the death of America. "How lamentable and disastrous it would be if what God intended as an incentive and a means to an appreciation of the higher things, the immortal and the eternal, should prove, through the lust of the flesh and the pride of the intellect, a malediction."

The action he took against a group which, in 1935, engaged Carnegie Hall for a huge demonstration to foster the dissemination of birth control methods and literature, received wide publicity. His sermon at St. Patrick's Cathedral, his subsequent theses in rebuttal (for the debate continued a long time) filled many columns in domestic and foreign newspapers. In those disquisitions he proved, if never before he had proved, the artistry of his oratory as a vehicle for the pronouncement of his logic, ethics, scholarship, and Catholic citizenship.

The people of New York City, including many of those not of his faith, figuratively cheered when they read his releases to the press. For, in presenting his argument, Cardinal Hayes used language and reasoning that no man or woman could fail to understand. He was addressing the public and he refrained from esoteric phrases, philosophic and theologic, that would have meant nothing to thousands. The birth control advocates at Carnegie Hall had based their argument on economic grounds. His Eminence answered on economic grounds, with quotations from economists which evidenced an unusual degree of scholarship.

Our economic ills, his opponents had contended, would surge higher if the birth rate were not cut down. In answer to this he said: "Remember also that the birth rate is seven hundred thousand fewer in one year, and that this deficit is constantly increasing. And remember too that this whole process is cumulative—something like compound interest in reverse. Is this the way to bring back prosperity? Is business to be improved by a constant, and even more rapid *constriction* of the market for all commodities? Will it help the unemployment situation by making it necessary to manufacture less and less goods? Will not the birth prevention movement in reality achieve the contraception of consumers and prosperity?"

One among his adversaries, the mother of a prominent motion picture actress, had suggested "voluntary sterilization" for those of the poor too ignorant to manage contraceptive methods. Cardinal Hayes spoke in a voice quivering with muffled anger as he came to this part of his opponents' platform: "Who are those people that sit in soft garments and offer affront to the poor? Are they a race apart, superior beings with a special commission to order the lives of others less fortunate in worldly goods than themselves? And the women among them, who would enjoin the poor from motherhood, are they taking over from the poor the privilege of motherhood because they are the better able to bear the burden? *You know they are not.*"

Parallel with his firm dicta on birth control were his unequivocal stands against prohibition and divorce. In all of these were the contention that they aimed to destroy the American family, American manhood, American spirituality. He was ever prompted in his thoughts, words, and deeds by the spirit of St. Paul, voiced in the words, "I live now; yet not I, but Christ liveth in me!"

America was to him the world in miniature; he saw it as a benediction and he intended to give his life to keeping it as such. He was the Catholic citizen in action, up and down the highways and by-ways of his diocese, lashing out at any who skulked in wait to ensnare the youth of the land. Not his to stand aloof with head turned from the world of action like a painted saint on stained-glass window. Christ was a man of action. Patrick Joseph Hayes was a follower of Christ.

Christ was the Hero he had worshipped from his boyhood, the Hero who had lived peacefully and Who in His Manhood brought peace to others, and promised peace after His death to all the men who walked the world. That peace could be bought by anyone wishing to pay the small price of good will in following the Figure all the way to the Tree of Life. At the foot of that Cross one received the baptism of desire. The only intolerance necessary was an intolerance toward unjust aggressors creeping up to desecrate the Fruit of that Tree.

Always, from the days when he ran through the cold of dawn to serve Mass, he wanted to be another Christ. Now he possessed the authority of Christ over the ministers of Christ. His name was Patrick; he had all the love of an Irishman within him. He had, also, the spirit of active repulsion against evil with which, as Bishop of Chaplains, he led his priests on in the work of carrying the peace of Christ wherever men strove, like some youthful Joseph— up and doing with the enemy at his door.

America rode the crest of industrial success. But he saw her spacious family life sinking as in a water hole on a desert. The foundations needed reinforcement. But he moved among his people with optimism, glorifying those whose decency never made the front pages of the press: "Entirely too little attention is paid to the activities of people who lead decent and orderly lives, and too much attention is paid to those who have wandered away from the paths of true Christianity. The newspapers devote too many columns of their space to the exploitation of vice and the unChristian activities of persons who offend against the sound and simple laws of morality."

His prayer for the nation's families was thus: "God grant that in this day of much religious indifference and moral laxity the desert wastes in the social and spiritual life of America may yield to the benediction of divine grace, lest our family life be a life builded upon sand."

Youth he heard criticized on every side. Yet his whole outlook on the future of the nation was wrapped up in the soundness of young men and women whose apparent waywardness or flippancy he attributed to the bad example of adults. "Basically the young men and women of today are just as sound morally as they were a century ago. Some of them have been led by the appeals of vanity to venture beyond the confines of harmless frivolity. These young people will ultimately react to the proper influences and contribute to the progress of the world as the good God intended them to do."

In this concept the Cardinal was a true prototype of the Christ he yearned to imitate, the Christ who said, "Suffer little children to come unto Me." No hounding of the immature, but "proper influences," would set them on the right path.

Radical thought and movements were having their day. He did not avoid the issue there, for he knew Christ had never side-stepped an instance of evil. Rather, his manifest courage, embraced by a serene sanctity, evidenced itself in charitable, optimistic treatment. The priesthood was the ultimate step in Hayes' career. As Shepherd of the largest individual flock within the Church he found the joyousness of the religious adventure supremely satisfying. Free thought attacked his personal idealism and he retaliated with words of confidence; his confidence was inspired by the fact that among his sheep there were nine colleges and a university training over twelve thousand boys and girls; and two hundred and sixty-six elementary schools caring for ninety-seven thousand children. All this, with scarcely a penny of endowment.

Radical thought? "The spirit of radicalism," he said, "will ultimately melt before the true influence of Christianity and will leave that part of the world which resisted it better off than it was before."

The man gloried in his work as a painter glories in a canvas well worth the feeling of exhaustion when the paint is dry. The work of this man took most of the hours of his day; but it was a role he loved, for he daily followed in the steps of his Hero. Indeed, he was the incarnation of the imitation of Christ! The joy of his life reached its peak of excitement when he said, "I live now; yet not I, but Christ liveth in me."

CHAPTER VI

DEMOCRACY'S ARISTOCRAT

IN the reasoning of Patrick Joseph Hayes no one group of people anywhere in the world possessed the prerogatives of democracy above any other group. He regarded the consideration of the United States as a democracy purely in the same sense that the people of the United States had decided to set for themselves a code of living conformable to the highest and most decent concepts which the human mind could evolve for the best and highest interests of the human soul. Body and soul are each a separate entity, each dependent on the other for its existence. Naturally, then, he devoted his physical and mental energies to the furthering of democracy as an aid to the life of men's souls. Their physical betterment would follow inevitably. What is good for the soul cannot help being good for the body.

Shepherd of a spiritual flock, organizer of economic, charitable programs, militant defender of his country's system of government, Patrick Cardinal Hayes saw in democracy a wider, vaster meaning than most world statesmen. Himself a statesman, senator of a body whose legislation far exceeded in lasting influence the daily law-making of secular assemblies, his vision embraced a dream of all men working in the co-operation of one family. This was his dream; but it was no idle, romantic illusion of a Utopia such as would appear ephemerally magnetic to the reader of a current best seller.

His dream lived, for it was not exactly a dream but a faith in an unquenchable reality. Millions pass through the great Catholic cathedrals of the world, genuflecting before the little tabernacles in each, kneeling before the altars, raising their heads to receive the little white Wafer in Which resides the supreme Aristocrat with Whom the millions of heaven's democrats all over the universe have come to commune. In the form of the Eucharist, the Aristocrat has mingled with the democrats, and when He has touched them and entered into their bodies, He has raised them, too, up to His own dignity. He has become part of them. It is the Shepherd living in Person among and within His sheep. It is the Master, the Ruler, giving Himself to His people. More, it is democracy attaining the plane of aristocracy through Him. God's promise thus becomes fulfilled. "If I be lifted up I will draw all things to Me."

This, then, was the concept which democracy took in the mind of Cardinal Hayes, who never ceased to thrill to the ecstasy which his priesthood brought him. "The mission of the Church," he always brought home to his flock, "is always the same —today, yesterday and forever—namely, to bring God to man and man to God, whether man be rich or poor, strong or weak, great or humble, contented or otherwise." The practice of Catholicism would be an empty, dead thing, a meaningless gesture, if its essential universality, its accessibility to all creatures through grace divine, were denied any one of them. In the secular sense of the word, aristocracy implies a "better than thou" attitude. Not so with His Master! There were no barriers separating Him from His people. When they were poor or sick, that was the time He went to them, loved them and helped them most. When they bore the brunt of social ostracism because of foul disease or sinfulness, He soothed them, fearing not to be seen in their company. This was His gentleness, His charity. This was the evidence of His aristocracy, for only the true aristocrat in dignity and character will go down to the lowly.

The Cardinal followed the simplicity of Christ and he reproduced in himself the Christ ideal. There was no room in his make-up for pomp or power or material ambition. There could have been no room for such desires in him, for his being, long before the honors of the Cardinalate had come to him, had been surcharged with all the enthusiasm of youth for an aspiration to receive the oils of Holy Orders. Full of the zest of life from his first days as a boy in his old Five Points birthplace, he knew but one Hero and he smiled his way till he reached his ambition—the priesthood of God, the ministry of Christ, the ultimate goal he had set for himself. The seriousness with which this purpose filled him only made him the more human, a logical and consistent effect since he was traveling the road, step by step, of the God who had Himself lived as a man among men. And this faithful following in the footsteps of the supreme Human Being led to Patrick Cardinal Hayes' becoming another Christ.

The humanity of Christ, His kindness, democratic spirit, peacefulness—all were blessedly contagious. This Divine humanity was caught up by the Cardinal of Charities even as a boy playing with his fellows. He had always been imbued with the Christlike qualities. When he was at school, his companions called him the "Pope," an epithet then in use by boys which they attributed to one who obviously was more devout than the rest, more prayerful, more serene. The spirit vibrated in him, making him deeper in thought and loftier in character as the years passed.

As time brought with it the promotion to higher office, he increased in his capacity for administering calmly, wisely, yet judiciously.

At this point we are reminded of the words of Pope Pius XI, "Many are raised to the dignity of God, and incorporated into the Mystical Body of Christ." Cardinal Hayes was raised to the dignity of God Incarnate when he became a priest. This was to him the supreme honor of all that could ever come to him. He accepted it with all that it meant to him, proceeding to that unity with the Holy

Trinity in the daily exercise of his privilege to change the nature of bread and wine into the substance of Christ's Body and Blood. Cognizant of this power, he yet remained the boy in spirit and tone, going about his priestly work with the same enthusiasm that had characterized him in youth as a lad of studious enterprise.

His priesthood gave him the opportunity he had always sought. It sent him into the lives of St. Gabriel's parishioners and later into the lives of the people in St. Stephen's. This was what he had been ordained for, this was the work he wanted to do, and he set himself to do it as Christ Himself would have done it. In him was the realization that he, one member of the millions of God creations, one democrat among all the sons of God, retained within him the power to be raised up to God because he lived in the knowledge that his strength came from Christ, the Divine Aristocrat. Not only was he spurred by this knowledge, but also by the knowledge that Christ lived within him as a Real Presence when he received Holy Communion; that he was a walking tabernacle holding in his heart the offspring of God, the Son of Mary, the Prince of Peace. It was as if his own mother had, before dying, promised him that although he would never again see her in this life, she would nevertheless stay alive, keep him company, whisper to him and encourage him from within his body for the rest of his life! With such realization, no man would mourn too much the death of his mother, beyond grieving that he must forbear the sight of her face. He would go the rounds of his duties, jubilant and confident, succeeding because his innate sorrow had turned to joy.

So was Cardinal Hayes the embodiment of peace and calm. So was he doubly ready to undertake the heavy responsibilities of his work as Cardinal when the time came for the Hero of his youth to reach out to draw him nearer to His side. The exalted position lent a prestige and world-wide fame which might have made a lesser man draw himself to full stature and stand proud, even arrogant. Power over men belonged to Cardinal Hayes; it was his to use so that those under his scepter might rise or fall at his command. But, instead, he accepted the position of the Prince of the Church, member in the Sacred College of Cardinals,—senator of a body of princes who exercised the power and the privilege of naming the Vicar of Christ on earth—in a spirit of humility and complete subjection to the Lord of the Universe. He was an aristocrat of the hierarchy. But he knew in his heart that the title of 'Cardinal,' or any other title, in itself, does not make a man an aristocrat. The Eucharist, Christ's coming to man in Body, Blood, Soul, and Divinity, is the great means by which the democracy of humanity becomes lifted up to the aristocracy of God. The Shepherd of New York unconsciously delineated his own self, nature, qualities, and measures of his diocesan administration as reflecting the love and interest Christ has in

His heart for men: "Lest the glory of the divinity and the majesty of kingship awe and terrify the children of men, Christ, through the Wisdom of the Father, presents Himself as the Shepherd King. He would rule the mind and heart of man with all the simplicity, kindliness, humility, and self-sacrifice of a shepherd. No room in His Sacred Heart for lust of power, tyranny of injustice, avarice of riches, that have all too regularly marked the rule of earthly princes."

In these words he gave utterance to his concept of His Majesty, the Son of God, Who emptied Himself of His glory in order that the élite of His creatures might be filled with divine dignity inherited.

CHAPTER VII

Militant Chaplain

NONE of Cardinal Hayes' qualities presents him in a clearer or more attractive light than the courage which sent him into action as a soldier in the Army of Christ. Patrick Hayes as a boy, we saw, chose for his universal hero Christ the Boy. He was his great Soldier Hero, fighting a war single-handed, without poison gases for weapons, but only a soft-spoken word and parable that enthralled thousands. His legions, drawn from the unlearned peasants and fisherfolk, were ready to elect Him their ruler, for they needed a man like Him. Too long had they crept in submission to the usurers and Pharisees, the unjust aggressors, whose counterparts still survive as modern despots, political overseers to whom the human lives and souls of their subjects are so many sources of revenue.

The Soldier Hero fought a quiet battle, only once raising the lash, when he exorcised the profaners in the Temple. The unjust invaders had made His house a rendezvous of thieves. A symbol of the Judgment! "Not through the portals of My kingdom may they enter who come with vice and foul tricks!" Here was the only intolerance Christ acknowledged: intolerance of the bully who would enter to make a sacrilege out of the sacred. It was the enemy working from within whom He cast out. Christ was, and is, the perpetuation of the Church Militant.

Into His militant body He has injected His generals. Patrick Cardinal Hayes was an illustrious general in His army. A general without a trained military body is impotent to carry out the campaign plans of the Commander-in-Chief. Consequently, the leader of the New York Archdiocese went to the camps, where Catholic soldiers are each year trained for the body militant, and delivered his message. His words rang with the vigor of a leader spurring his men and women to sustained action, drive and courage, in the fight that would take their whole lives to win.

"The mission of the Church," he said, "is never finished so long as the evil spirit is abroad in the world." Not merely in the land. In the world! The battle surges in the open field and in the hidden lane. "Against this spirit the Church carries on an unceasing warfare in the presence of her Bishops, priests, Religious and laity."

Christ the Conqueror had made the world His domain, conquering it by the Cross. But He had left a leader in the field, even as a general leaves his aide when he retires. His leader cannot, *may not,* fail. He has seen to that. And the Cardinal, worthy helpmate of the Vicar in one of the farflung fields of that militant legion, pointed to him as the zest-

ful delegate of the Spiritual Kingdom: "We look
in vain, in our day, for Peter, unmistakably the head
and foundation of the Church according to Holy
Scripture, if we ignore, or fail to accept, his suc-
cessor in the person of Pope Pius XI, whose universal jurisdiction in spiritual matters is unique,
compared to all others, as it operates unconfiined by
merely national, racial, linguistic, and territorial
divisions of the human race. Such universal head-
ship alone can guarantee Christian unity."

And the Auxiliary-Bishop Hayes was himself
to be designated as one enjoying a similar jurisdiction, universally, as Chaplain Bishop over all of
America's soldier priests fighting for their democracy that Christ's kingdom might remain intact on
this earth. He was the only man in America ever
to have enjoyed the position. It had in it a suggestion
of the reach of the Papacy.

"The Church, Our Holy Mother," he never
ceased to remind us, "is so desirous to see the Kingdom of Christ spread on earth and to carry on that
mighty battle for the Lord, that one of her greatest
weapons, her very essential weapon—in fact, absolutely necessary—must be our universities, colleges,
academies, and elementary schools."

These were the training camps of the legions
of decency, forging, not tanks and motorized muni-
tions, but souls and minds impregnable in the face
of the enemy. He pleaded for Ignatiuses from among
the men, for Joans of Arc from among the women.

The quest of Galahad is our quest. The Holy Grail is still to be sought by every knight who has been dubbed a soldier of Christ at Confirmation.

"May we ask you, in this year of graduation and the years which will follow, to go out as apostles and ministers of the Eucharist, and by your lives and examples show your faith, your deep love, your yearning desire to have others love and serve Christ likewise!" So he pleaded for the enlistment of youth.

His warfare was not strife against a race or despot for imperialistic aggrandizement. It was not one of the periodic conflicts that break out in the history of every epoch. What he considered enemies were clearly the spites and malices, petty hatreds, bigotries, lusts of the flesh, and lusts for material gain which crowd around men and women, both old and young. "The enemy of the flock is the wolf. Its savage cruelty strikes terror into the human heart. Christ has no defense for the protection of the fold other than Himself. He carries but a shepherd's staff. But His Own Divine Person, without barrier or armor of man's making, keeps in safety the sheep that hear His voice and follow Him." The voice is gentle. The Cardinal was gentle.

The forces of the material have ever eaten deep into the consciousness of men. The lure savored of easy living, fewer responsibilities, greater luxury. The wolf was the modern free thinker, the birth controller, the communistic "ideologist," suavely walking through the society of Christianity. Christ was the sole enemy. He had to go before these marauders could get a toe hold; and the easiest way to erase Him was to get His own soldiers to revolt within the ranks. But the Bishop, the shepherd, also walked in the society of Christianity and stood guard against invasion of the fold. More, he was up early and administered immunizing vaccine before the wolf could reach his flock.

His words were the encouraging words of a doctor telling a patient how to keep well. "With Him and His who abide with Him, there is no fear of the wolf that symbolizes the spirit of hatred, injustice, sensuality, and domination among nations and individuals, and begets crime against society and the scourge of war with all the terror that accompanies it."

But when the time came for the enemy to break out in no longer subtle, but vicious, attack, he was eager to spike down the molester. When the enemy had entered the house of God, Christ lashed about Him with a whip. Christianity was the great mansion of God built upon the fertile estate of His earth. The unjust aggressor had dared to invade the peaceful lives of men whose bodies could know no peace in the turmoil he had caused in their souls. The spiritual battle had broadened and become a holocaust. To save the soul of the world, it was necessary to purge the body.

Said the future Cardinal Hayes, referring to the position of the Catholic Church on war: "Our

three great wars could have had no higher ideals.
The War of Independence was fought for the principle of self-government, self-determination for the
right of a people to determine its road of destiny,
progress, and national aspirations. The Civil War
led out of the bondage of slavery a race of human
beings and sealed a union of sovereign States, one
and inseparable. The last war overseas drew our
American soldiers into its awful vortex of suffering
and death in order that no government, no people,
might be permitted by superior brute force to en-
slave another nation and deprive that nation of its
right and opportunity for self-determination, self-
growth, and self-government; and that American
ideals of national life and conduct and hope might
not be threatened by an empire of blood and iron."

In keeping with the position of the Church,
he expressed also the Church's intolerance of paci-
fists who refuse to take arms against those who would
despoil our inherent rights and properties, even in-
directly. "There is a mission here in New York for
every one who loves New York and America. Here
we find enemies, men and women, trying to tear
out the very life of our country, and we who are
loyal to the flag must work for America first, last,
and all the time, for by helping America, we help
the entire world."

This was his concept of the breadth of human
society. Each man's house is his home, inviolable.
Each town and village is his home's home and must

be protected as man would safeguard the shelter he sleeps beneath. House and town; town and city; city, state, and nation; nations, domains, kingdoms—yea, the whole world is a man's home. Communism, atheism, social injustice, birth control, prohibition, obscene literature, bigotry (oral and in the press), immorality on the stage and on the screen, divorce, political despotism, racial prejudice, crime, radicalism in the schools, these were the enemies Cardinal Hayes found striking at the heart of democracy and he made haste to slay them.

He knew that Christ had been submissive through all His gory persecution. Yet the Sign of the Cross is today the sign of His Empire. Christ's submission was the manifestation of what Divine Love could do. His suffering He tolerated to show men what they could endure with His strength inside them. He had emptied Himself of His glory and let His persecutors do what they had pleased. He is the perpetuation of the Church Militant and He conquered with Peace.

These were the lessons the Cardinal learned and lived. His own message to his people paralleled the Master's. He was the understudy of Christ, the Alter Christ, giving his sheep the blessing of Christ, the Sign of the Cross. With the sign of peace he led them to do battle, but never to intimidate the other sheep who were not of his fold. Bigotry he despised; both the bigotry of the poor, ignorant intolerants outside the Church who tried to stamp it out by their petty speeches and tracts, and the bigotry that Catholics sometimes harbor towards those who labor without the benefit of light. To these Catholics he said, "Christ's government of His sheepfold differs radically from that of all other ruling. He preserves the unity and solidarity of His vast flocks, not as a common mass, group, or multitude, but by His solicitude for the humblest and the most insignificant in the fold. Where is it recorded that any other king has so loved his people that he has gone in search of the erring and missing ones as the Good Shepherd has done? Christ leaves the ninety and nine in the desert to go after the one that is lost, 'and when He hath found it, lays it upon His shoulders rejoicing.' "

When vilification came to the Church and her Holy Family during days of moral bankruptcy, Cardinal Hayes came to her defense much as Our Lord defended Himself in the face of the self-loving Pharisees: without floridness, temper or rage. He said on one occasion: "Outrageous attacks, through pulpit and printed word, were made on the Divinity of Christ and the Virgin Birth. It is, indeed, in some respects, a tribute to the Babe and His Mother, that all the heresy, schism, rationalism, agnosticism, and atheism of these nineteen centuries have utterly failed to take from them their sway over the minds and souls of millions and millions of men. . . Let me say, however, that, as these shocking and deplorable assaults have increased, there has been a corresponding growth in the fervor of the devotion and the strengthening of the faith of our own Catholic people toward Christ and His Mother."

Thus spake the Alter Christus, Patrick Cardinal Hayes, man, shepherd, Hero-worshipper of Christ, in the role of apostle, militant leader in the Militant Body of the Army of Christ.

We have spoken of his assignment as Chaplain-Bishop of all Catholic chaplains during the war. Of the latter there were more than a thousand. Here was a prelate of the Church holding authority over those who fought in two armies at once: the army of their country and the army of Christ. Their duty to the state had double significance, for the success of a nation's armed forces depends entirely upon the spirit, the zest, the morale of its men. And who but the chaplains inspired that morale, and kept up hope and confidence by the proximity of the King of Kings? With death so near, what folly to fight for a mere temporary victory! But to fight with the Divine Kingdom a gasp away! That was something to go into battle for.

And the designation Auxiliary-Bishop Hayes received from Pope Benedict XV on November 29, 1917, was the appointment to be Catholic Bishop Ordinary of the Armed Forces of the United States. His Vicar-General was Monsignor George J. Waring, whose untiring aid and executive ability in the organization that soon was to follow lived for the remainder of his days in the Cardinal's memory.

In an address to His Grace in the name of all chaplains of the Army and Navy he said: "It affords us special satisfaction to feel that the organization, which you developed so wonderfully and so rapidly in the Diocesis Castrensis, has largely contributed to demonstrate your ability to handle the complex problems, which must necessarily arise in so large a diocese as New York. Your appointment has been made only after due consideration of your fitness and qualifications, as proved by your work as Chaplain-Bishop. . . When you assumed charge of the work, things were in a chaotic state. Millions of men were being mobilized for the war and the Church had no organization nor machinery for coping with the problems which daily became more complicated. The government was calling for large numbers of priests, and it was difficult for the country at large to appreciate the urgent need for prompt action. . . When passing through New York to the war center, individually or collectively, the chaplains were received by you at your home. You inspired them with the highest priestly ideals, by your fatherly, sympathetic, and encouraging words."

This was a tribute that any man would welcome from his chief of staff. Monsignor Waring also said: "In February, 1918, when you actively took up your work as Chaplain-Bishop, there was only a handful of priests in our army and navy. When the armistice was signed in November, 1918, you had the largest diocese in the world. . . On the latter

THE CATHOLIC CHAPLAIN-BISHOP AND FATHER DUFFY

CARDINAL HAYES
from the portrait by Sir John Lavery in Fordham University

date, there were three and a half million soldiers and sailors in the service and you had fifteen hundred priests already serving in camps in America and Europe, or awaiting appointment. . . Your five vicariates included the Philippines, Hawaiian Islands, Alaska, the United States, Panama, Porto Rico, Ireland, England, France, Italy, Belgium, Germany, and Russia. . . Those of us long familiar with military and naval affairs, consider it to be a most remarkable achievement during the war, that you had your hand constantly on the pulse of the work which was being done by your priests and Catholic welfare organizations, in every section of your almost world-wide diocese. No wonder, then, when I was in Rome recently, the Holy Father and the Cardinals of the Consistorial Congregation expressed to me in most glowing terms their admiration of your phenomenal organization and administrative ability. It is not astonishing, therefore, that when the Church needed a Bishop, specially qualified and tried, to govern the important diocese of New York, you were selected. . . We pray . . . that you may continue to reflect honor and credit on our Church, our country, your diocese, and yourself."

Just how well Patrick Cardinal Hayes participated in the answering of that prayer has since become one of the most glorious pages in the history of New York.

Two priests, two chaplains, two friends occupy

shining positions in these glorious pages. During the war The Chaplain-Bishop of all American Catholic chaplains will in memory forever be associated with Francis Patrick Duffy.

From their seminary days in St. Joseph's, both men were inseparable friends; they were happy companions when time permitted them to exchange heart secrets. They had many things in common. Both were born relatively poor, but in atmospheres of refinement and spiritual culture. There was native dignity in their homes, engendered by the God-fearing parents and foster parents who reared them. Father Duffy often said that in his home, in Coburg, Canada, among his brothers and sisters, he found the environment itself an educational institution where all the children were virtually surrounded by the classics. His father had been a mill worker, faithful to his position as head of a large family. He had the evanescence of fun which transplanted itself in the laughing eyes of his priest son. His mother gave him his nobility of mold in brow, and penetration talents. Just as Cardinal Hayes had been the focal point of his aunt and uncle's life— the two becoming more devoted to each other because of their common devotion to the boy, Patrick —so was Francis Duffy, the boy, the incarnation of his mother's heart and intellect.

The friendship between the two men was inevitable, perhaps ordained by God Who was the Hero of them both. Christ to them was the Champion of the world, rising head and shoulders over all the heroes of history's arena. Besides, He meant more than merely a passing figure of conquest. He the Lord of Creation was to both a personal friend, Who, after creating all things, came in person to save His handiwork with His own Blood.

Naturally, then, as young seminarians, their outlook on life was the same. Francis Duffy was attracted to the quiet, keen intelligence of Patrick Hayes, aspiring to be like him in his manhood. Serenity was then, as it was throughout his mature years in the administrative exercise of diocesan duties, the future Cardinal's main characteristic in any sort of enterprise or crisis. His poise lent him the suggestion of the dignitary. Natural endowments in simplicity of heart caused him to impress others as a serious-minded man, willing to help them in their problems. Though he was serious minded, he never took himself seriously.

On the occasion of Father Duffy's tenth anniversary as Chaplain of the Sixty-ninth Regiment and Silver Jubilee as Army Chaplain, the Cardinal referred back "to those days when he (Father Duffy) was a very nice young priest and I was a very nice young priest, too. . . And when we tried to solve the problems of life by philosophy, little did we dream then that the gods had mapped out our careers such as they did. I have said publicly before that I never dreamed: I could never dream in those days, when I had this wise, scholarly priest alongside me, that he should have stepped out of cloister and become a man of war, a man like that to be called on to offer his birthright at the cannon's mouth. . . I know his honest opinion of me then was that I would never make a Bishop, much less a Cardinal. Yes, we talked much in those days, and we saw life, saw the future of America, because of the deep, profound scholarship, which is a grace that Father Duffy has not been able to unfold to the public. That brought to my mind on many occasions the philosophy of history, and in our talks together we would go over the facts, we talked of what America did for the world in general in its great institutions of democracy. We talked of its dangers, we talked of its opportunities, but little did I dream then that this good priest of God would play such an important part in the making of the world safe for democracy."

Cardinal Hayes in characteristic humility always looked up to Father Duffy. Even in the seminary he insisted that Father Duffy was his intellectual superior. Later he made him his advisor and counsel, discussing with him his opportunities and duties as Chaplain-Bishop. He saw the "Fighting Chaplain" as a great source of morale, especially to those of Irish ancestry, who looked up to him as an ideal of romantic chivalry, garbed as a priest and withal the living entity of glorious manhood.

In later life, of course, their paths led them somewhat apart in the field of Christ's work on earth. The prelate was confined to indoor, desk and office, routine—statistics, policies, trends, and movements. Father Duffy was the hale and hearty man among the people, living in an atmosphere of less formal ceremony than his friend. He loved men and life, and on this subject once said: "The thing about human life most impressive to one like myself, who does not belong to any one social class but has a natural affiliation with all of them, is that everybody is a human being. David Harum had it about right: 'There is as much human nature in some folks as there is in others, if not more.' . . . For myself, I cannot claim any special attribute except that of being fond of people—not this kind of people or that kind of people—just people. The object of civilization, it seems to me, is to cultivate a set of human beings who are at least tolerant of each other in everything that is not destructive, and at the same time to leave room for the cultivation of particular interests or enthusiasms. . . I stand with the class of people that by birth and association I belong to and move in the directions of organized labor and social reform."

Father Duffy's humane congeniality stands side by side with that of Cardinal Hayes. The former had set his heart on a career as a metaphysician; indeed, he once taught metaphysics at the seminary. But life found for him a more active opportunity to bestow on men his great working sympathy for them. He commented that ". . . we are all strongly united in the determination to defend and maintain the basic principles of American life. To pass on to future generations the American spirit of tolerance, broad-mindedness and liberality, to make prevail more and more that spirit in life which, whether it be known as democracy, fraternity or charity, is the loveliest endowment of human nature."

Not only did he hold such principles: his life proved that he practiced them, even as his Chaplain-Bishop, the Cardinal of Charities, practiced them. Their common interest lay in the welfare of the poor, the development of America, of human beings in general. Both men were writers and scholars, orators of wide influence and, above all, both exercised a keen influence on the youth of America and Christendom. To live so that youth would see in them the vital meaning of the priesthood and to stimulate in youth the desire for the priesthood as one of the manliest careers in life—that was the aim of both. That they achieved their end is a matter of history.

Both Father Duffy and Cardinal Hayes were to a degree masked men to the public. But statesmen, men in business, and politicians came to them for advice. Among these were members of all creeds, all sects, no creeds, no sects; but they were men who knew they needed guidance and they knew that Father Duffy and Cardinal Hayes understood men and would talk things over with them.

Neither was herculean; both were delicate.

Father Duffy suffered from the fever he contracted while working among veterans of the Spanish-American War. The Cardinal was small in stature, yet massive in the amount of stored energy he concealed; a man of great will power in driving himself to use that energy.

When these two friends visited each other, they found mutual delight. They relaxed in conversation at the rectory of Holy Cross Church in Forty-second Street or at the Cardinal's residence. There was not the slightest suggestion on Father Duffy's part of anything like forgetfulness of the amenities due his ecclesiastical and military superior; there was nothing of the unwarrantably familiar in the chaplain's attitude; but neither was there any trace of his being unconscious of his friend's exalted rank. The Cardinal always addressed his friend as "Frank" when they met in these informal hours, but the latter avoided the use of any kind of title or name in his conversations with the prelate.

In these intimate sessions the hunger in the Cardinal's heart for local color stories could be sensed in the readily released chuckle or sigh as his loyal comrade in the service of God and country talked. His yarns served to satisfy the common concept of the comic or eccentric that these human prelates held for men who took themselves a bit too seriously.

After nearly an hour of this sort of light exchange, their mood changed. Current problems took the floor. The freedom and prosperity of Holy Mother Church in her relations to the American or foreign systems of government were discussed with a gravity that revealed their unuttered and mutually held aspirations. Seldom was there any mention of the Holy Name as they conversed. But there were frequent quotations from St. Augustine, Saint Francis, and St. Thomas Aquinas that could be applied to the problems at hand. These scholastic authorities usually confirmed their position by quoting Christ in word and deed. The two men, whose days were spent in the busy city, were ever conscious of Christ as the Bond eternal whose dominion over their every thought, word, and deed made them exchange a devotion for each other. It was a devotion presenting a clear reflection of the Prince of their hearts' peace, gladdening their days among men, in the least or greatest of whom each saw his Master.

To Father Duffy his ecclesiastical chief was a man who could be an intimate of any of his subordinates without the slightest compromise in official and canonical demands or decorum. He looked up to Cardinal Hayes as a monumental figure symbolizing common sense allied with balanced initiative in administrative action. The Cardinal's priestliness appealed to him above all. That the prelate had grown older in precious experience but younger in buoyancy of heart and broadening interests, was a comment often heard on Father Duffy's lips.

Furthermore, he frequently cited the prelate's official actions illustrating his talent for seeing problems in a panorama that envisioned the present and the distant future.

He saw him as a man capable of truly catholic or universal love for mankind, in defeat as well as in victory. He would often say that Patrick Joseph Hayes was a dignitary on his Ordination day, who gracefully outgrew the manner of the preferred as he ascended rung by rung the ladder of ecclesiastical preferment.

There was always a lesson in the democracy born of manly humility when the two men, holding places of exceptional honor, exchange estimates of each other. Repeatedly, this Prince of the Church expressed his appreciation of Father Duffy's extraordinary stature among his intellectual contemporaries, evincing the sincerity of his eulogies by requesting Father Duffy to act as his adviser when he was preparing a document on education or Church and State relations. In the role of one coming for advice, Cardinal Hayes reminds one of the boy at the feet of a preceptor, as he laid before the Chaplain of the Fighting Irish knotty problems he faced as Catholic Chaplain General of the army and navy. They would put their heads together as associates with a common ideal of service to the nation in a crisis, and exchange views and convictions. They were soldiers of Christ making the world safe for Christianity.

In the matter of politics their attitude was

similar. Their great capacities for affection for all men of sincerity enjoined them from bias in judging the intrinsic and humanitarian merits of political party legislation. Their faith in political leaders could only be dampened by the conviction that a candidate's interest in serving himself superseded his sworn duty to the people. Such information they were in a position to keep up to date.

It was a delight to be present when they compared the relative stature of history's departed luminaries. Here they were capable of the boy's enthusiasm for great men without lapsing into idolatry.

When Father Duffy returned from the war he met Archbishop Hayes in the latter's residence, April 23, 1919. A warmth of greeting permeated the atmosphere, electric with spontaneous informality. There were no ecclesiastic amenities, no military demands of authority and subordination. Rather, they were like two boys with many stories to tell each other about a great adventure just completed. The one had been in the thick of the fight; the other had remained behind the scenes planning and organizing.

Father Eugene J. Callahan, when president of the Cathedral College Alumni, arranged for them to be guests of honor at an Alumni reunion banquet. At the dinner Archbishop Hayes was presented with a Cappa Magna by the Alumni, Father Callahan acting as spokesman.

Father Duffy brought greetings of the Army

and veterans. In the speech he was called on to make his theme rang with the universal joy which the whole army had felt in Archbishop Hayes' singular office as Chaplain-Bishop of the American Army and Navy. The fact that Rome had so honored him, Father Duffy said, registered a double adulation. It showed the whole country what strength and moral guidance were embraced in the retiring figure of the Archbishop who was called upon to direct the activities of all the chaplains of America, no matter what land or sea they might have been ordered to.

Cardinal Hayes and Father Duffy both had the same healthy appetite for friendships, but there was a contrast in their methods of accumulating such treasures. Father Duffy was the man to go after his game, always ready with a humorous story. Putting people at their ease had its effect in eliciting from them jocular commentaries.

The Cardinal, schooled in the study and application of canonical niceties of deportment and in the demands of parliamentary procedure traditional in ecclesiastical routine, was of necessity the delighted observer of life's levities as they came within his ken. He had to await the haphazard contact with figures currently engaging the eye of the public. It was a welcome taste of holiday relaxation when the priest of cosmopolitan contacts brought to his residence such men as Will Rogers, George M. Cohan, Irving S. Cobb.

These interludes he treasured in his large capacity for the fun of the hour. They balanced his life, made him forget temporarily affairs of state, and sent him back to his work refreshed. They lived in his mind, too, as the sources of choice remarks to add to his native repertoire of wit which he shared daily with his staff.

As their lives passed through the tremendous history of the twentieth century, each man taking his place in the seriousness of the era, opportunities of getting together to philosophize or quip were all too few. By training and lifelong habit, both were given to evaluating all men's greatness by comparing men's works and words with the revealed Mind and Heart of Christ. The Master continued through their lives as a Mystical Presence ever at their sides. They were nothing less than glib in questioning the Church Fathers in their interpretations of Christ's utterances as applied to current problems. The justice and rights of international claims were submitted to Scriptural treatment of like principles before either man would venture a personal conviction as to the ethics or legality of the disputants.

It was in their occasional exchange of immediate reactions to Christ that these two men of affairs revealed to each other new growth in their affections for the Master Whose divine humility tolerated lovingly their wordless professions of loyalty. They would welcome death as the supreme evidence of their uncompromising sincerity. As a result, they were blessed in a consciousness of an everdeepening friendship for each other, fostered by recurring revelations—even in the days of late middle age—of devotional capacities in each other hitherto undiscovered.

Their common desire to serve their God, the divine Chief of the Church Militant, was another source of deep friendship. Father Duffy had nurtured from boyhood the hope of being an active apostle in camp and on battlefield. The romance in his soul gave strength to his determination to seek adventure in the defense of Christian ideals where the fight for right would take place. The huge drama he desired was unacceptable unless it ignored completely the cost to self.

But Auxiliary-Bishop Hayes found in his experiences as an organizer his best medium for service to Church and State in wartime. His prayer that he be given opportunity to serve in the conflict as a true minister of Mother Church's Sacramental graces was answered in the form of the official assignment by Archbishop Farley to be the latter's representative, and that of the National Catholic War Council in mobilizing and assigning volunteers of the priesthood to posts of service in camps here and abroad.

This common role of chaplain was another bond between Patrick Hayes and Francis Duffy. First through personal conferences, and later through correspondence, they were collaborators in zealous work in the interest of the morale of a militant America. Father Duffy later said: "Archbishop Hayes is a human being—and more than just a human being. The Archbishop of New York has the heart of a boy. Everybody has been touched today by the delightful human quality of his kindly reminiscences of me. His position has not changed him. He is as democratic as Al Smith!"

The warm love of America for these men, who mingled with the nation's citizens and officials of all faiths and party affiliations, is a justification of their deeply implanted optimism toward humanity as a whole. Well might the egotists abroad, usurping the seats of the mighty, look to Columbia as the great teacher of something higher and nobler than mere tolerance!

CHAPTER VIII

Heritage of Faith

THE Shepherd of New York, proud of the land of nativity and proud, too, of his Irish ancestry, said: "I am conceited enough to think that no better American lives than myself. Equally am I convinced that I am the better American because I am Irish, and the better Irishman, because I am an American."

It is characteristic of the Irish that they have always been grateful for the opportunity of coming to this country in the hour of their need. The American Constitution gave to these lovers of liberty and happiness the chance to develop their innate capacity for freedom and the pursuit of happiness.

America was the land beyond the horizon for them. It was indeed the promised land. It was what they had prayed for through the centuries and they were willing to fight for it and develop it so that it would yield a fine harvest. The basis of Irish happiness always lay in a field they could plow, with their eyes on the stars, and a bit of a home where their babes could dream of the angels.

Like the promise of the Star of Bethlehem to the Wise Men, a new phrase was emblazoned over the world—"Life, liberty, and the pursuit of happiness!" The Irish responded to that invitation with characteristic verve. It was a feast they could do justice to. It was a feast to which they would carry the bounty of their birthright. The banquet hall was vast and spacious, and it needed their resonant notes of laughter and song. Pent up within their hearts were the notes of lyre and harp, awaiting release like a skylark in a cage.

The Irish immigrants came to the feast of happiness and liberty on the wide stretches of American soil. Their bodies and souls became nourished to the full; and they set about giving thanks, showing they were worthy guests. The ring of their axes filled the air. America was the land of joy and the Irish found it a land where the joyous life could find fulfillment.

Such was the spirit in which Cardinal Hayes' father and mother, aunt and uncle, had crossed the Atlantic. Daniel and Mary Hayes, poor in the worldly concept, rich in Catholic optimism, gave to America the dearest gift they had. Their son became a Prince of the Church and his Irish blood ran riot in his uncompromising battle against everything menacing to the welfare of America.

Aunt Ellen and Uncle Jim, who brought him up, transplanted into their American-born nephew the seeds of Irish faith, hope, and charity. He lived and matured under the influence of Irish breeding in the care of the Egans, who walked in the fear of the Lord and were good. They knew the sweetness of Christ. They were aware of their divine Benefactor's promise of eternal life and, therefore, took no chances of losing the reward.

Patrick Joseph Hayes throughout his lifetime was loyal to the ideals the Egans had inculcated in him. They had had the Irishman's concept of Catholic worship before God as the primary occupation of humanity; consequently, it was consistent in them that they should transfer to their nephew the real importance and significance of that concept. It was a principle made real, concrete, for it was to be embodied in a human being.

Cardinal Hayes definitely embraced the principle. The figure of Christ he followed from his earliest days: walking in the path of the obedient Boy in Nazareth; resisting the flesh and the devil; caring for the sheep in his fold; feeding and clothing the poor; educating the lowly; fasting and meditating; rising vigorously against the enemy from within and without; loving and making life happy for the little foundlings, even as Christ had suffered the little ones to come unto Him.

He was a genuine hero-worshipper; his Hero was Christ. His concept of hero-worship was that of the true Irishman, whose conduct glorifies God on high. The chivalrous feeling of the Irish lay deep within him and he remained a symbol of purity, never allowing the element of immorality to stalk into his fold. Yet Christ had not dealt harshly with His murderers while hanging on the Cross. And

Cardinal Hayes was vastly human in his loving optimism toward men. He knew their weaknesses and sins, but he was always ready and willing to grant them forgiveness. This was the heritage of Christ's priesthood flowering within this priest whose very humility brought him to an exalted position among the priests of God.

In all the realm of literature there was no figure as dramatic in the eyes of Cardinal Hayes as that of the crucified Christ. No words ever spoken were more fraught with the essence of nobility than the phrase, "Father, forgive them; for they know not what they do!" This was the basic formula of all human charity. These were the words which Cardinal Hayes kept hearing; they were like a message, a plea, and he listened to them and answered the plea. The Irishman within him, beautified by the iridescence of Catholicity, shone forth in the kindness and warmth which compelled the world to salute him as a commanding figure who led without commanding.

He never forgot that the blood of the Celt coursed through his veins. He never lost sight of the fact that Ireland had been a great factor in the successful growth of this new land, as it had aided in the growth and flourishing of other lands throughout the universe. His mental vision was peopled with millions of men and women who had gone forth from the Emerald Isle to make the countries of their settlement better places to live in. In his own words: ". . . not merely the little sorrowful Emerald Isle of the North Atlantic, but the Great Erin, the land of the Celt's dispersion, measured by the four corners of the world, reaching over the seven seas, unto continents and islands afar." His very language has the lilt, even in its prose, of the poets of Ireland. It sings itself, for it fits a rhythm and a melody.

His tribute to Ireland's gift to posterity was summed up in these words: "The tents of Ireland's exiled children are pitched in every land under the sun. The rare gifts and rich talents of her sons, denied opportunity on their own native soil, have found splendid and undying expression in successful and distinctive achievement all over the world." He spoke these words as an American, but he also spoke them in the spirit of a boy who praises his big brother, or his father, for his feats. Actually, in this speech Cardinal Hayes' words included himself, although it is recorded nowhere that he ever referred to his own accomplishments.

Nevertheless, the Cardinal himself was one of those sons whose "rare gifts and rich talents . . . found splendid and undying expression in successful and distinctive achievement all over the world." He is a monument to the land of saints and scholars. His expansive abilities bore fruit in the fields of education, economics, legislation, and sociology. He was a democrat of the world, who gazed out on the world and saw it needed adjustment. Its lowly needed succoring and he set about granting that aid. This was the broadness of the Irishman thinking within him and showing itself in his words and actions. It was the expansiveness of his Irish heart that brought him to organize Catholic Charities. Through all his maneuvers, however, his loyalty to the Cross of Christ, the shadow of which has always been over Ireland, never diminished.

His boyishness portrayed him as a challenge to the glum, gloomy piety which is a perverted notion of goodness. Sunny Irish optimism radiated from him, and filled him with the desire to go through his days lightheartedly, yet seriously mindful of the duties he owed to God and man.

In one of his utterances there is found this summing up of his concept of Ireland as a human symbol, of Ireland regarded as a person: "On the stage of the world's history, Erin has played many parts. She has been, in the highest sense, saint and scholar, apostle and priest, sage and soldier, bard and poet, prince and prisoner, exile and martyr." Not often do we come upon one who has been so much.

Unconsciously, he gave in these words a self-portrait. No one who has lived and worked with Cardinal Hayes will contradict this statement. Those who have followed his public career as a minister of the Faith, as a shepherd of his flock, as a guardian of the morals and manners of a city, as a Chaplain-Bishop of all the military priests of America, as an orator, educator, organizer, senator of the Church's

Sacred College of Cardinals, will not fail to see him in each of the roles he has attributed to Erin.

Considering the mystical sphere which the Church of Christ embodies, we may place him rightly as a prisoner, exile and martyr. He was an exile from eternity in the same sense that Lazarus was an exile from eternity when our Lord called him back from his heavenly reward. Lazarus had finished his mission on earth. A good man, he had passed from his term as a member of the Church Militant to his place among the members of the Church Triumphant (or at least to the Church Suffering in Purgatory). Christ's human kindness recalled him to appease the sorrow of his sisters, Mary and Martha. It was the Divine Will that Lazarus come back to earth.

Patrick Cardinal Hayes remained a member of the Church Militant for many years, practicing good works, meditating, battling the enemy, at all times an exile from eternity. Always, however, he extended himself to do the will of God. The greater his efforts, the higher his place in the realm of saints.

Some of the poetry of the Cardinal flows through this excerpt from one of his sayings: "The stars at night keep eternal vigil unto the Resurrection Morn over the final bivouac of her warrior dead, heroes fallen asleep on nearly every battlefield of medieval and modern times. A French historian tells us that, within fifty years after the fatal

1691, four hundred thousand Irish soldiers died on the battlefields of France. . . In every nook and cranny of Christendom the footprints of Ireland's missionaries, saints and scholars can be vividly traced by historic monuments of religion and civilization."

His keen appreciation of Erin's gift to the universe he expressed when he said: "Ireland steps out of the pages of time, a pathetic figure—noble, unique, mysterious, spiritual, and immortal."

Another poetic statement he made regarding Ireland shows the wide human sympathy he harbored for the activities and accomplishments of others: "Wherever and whenever the rising sun of humanity and justice appeared among nations, Erin was ready to serve the cause of freedom against tyranny, no matter what the sacrifice. Her sons have valiantly gone and borne in large measure the burden and heat of the day for others. Over the western ocean, in the crimson glory of the parting day, she has visioned the shores and gates of a land of promise, verily a city of God."

Here is the expression of his own gratitude for God's gift, America. Here, also, is Cardinal Hayes, the Irish-American, penetrating into the roots of America and glorying in what those roots have given life to. The soul of Ireland has been tried by fire and never has it been consumed. The relations of Ireland to America have always been close. The reciprocal contributions of both have gone into the

annals of history as evidence of what two countries
can do for one another when both are inspired by
the ideals of spirituality.

Concerning their reciprocal contributions, Cardinal Hayes said: "The contribution of America to
Ireland and of Ireland to America is great. Especially is this true when we bear in mind that there
has been a mutual and abiding contribution of all
that is best and all that counts from America to Ireland and from Ireland to America. 'Neither things
present nor things to come, neither height nor
depth, nor might nor right,' can ever possibly destroy the fact of this intimate relation."

Just what that "relation" means is not some
military combination to serve as an "axis" in time
of war. It is not a trade treaty for material aggrandizement, or a secret pact to conquer other nations.
If it were built merely on a material foundation, it
would be perishable and therefore worthless. Cardinal Hayes struck the correct note when he ana-
lyzed its true character thus: "It is through the soul
of Erin alone that we shall comprehend, in a measure, the integrity, the perpetuity, the continuity,
and the sublimity of her national ideals. The world
has seldom looked on the like before. Military
might, mastery of the sea, conquest of commerce are
not her kingdom. To her they mean, as they have
nearly always meant, tyranny, piracy, and a condition of servitude."

The chief factor, he pointed out, of Ireland's

contagious spirit lies in her Catholicity. The two definitions of this word are applied: first, Catholicity in a religious sense; secondly, in the sense of universality.

"The confines of this all-embracing Catholic spirit are coterminous with the bounds of the earth, and touch the very precincts of Heaven itself. By the North Star of faith in God and His all-wise Providence, Erin has fixed her course in fidelity and loyalty, and has never swerved. Under the Southern Cross, in exile and penal colony, her soul has been tried by fire, but has never been consumed."

Patrick Joseph Hayes inherited from Ireland the intense spirit of militancy mingled with the fervent spirit of sympathy for the human. His sincerity was born of Irish parentage, for his ready compliment came from the heart. His optimism was both Irish and Catholic; but it was not an optimism steeped in gullibility. His joyousness, wit, humor, love of laughter, lack of sophistication, maternal sweetness, are all part of Ireland's gift to America. It is also the Church's gift to America, for Ireland contributed his parents, and his aunt and uncle, to New York.

Patrick Cardinal Hayes was one with Joyce Kilmer in the latter's thought, "Romantic Ireland is not dead."

CHAPTER IX

AMERICA'S PRINCE

THE title of "prince" suggests to most of us a person of aloof dignity, to the manner born, as well as to the manor, while receiving homage, and exercising the authority which goes with his position. We think of a prince as a stately, unbending figure, a man born into a life of ease, heir to vast estates, and entitled to exemption from the ordinary routine of work.

There functions in the world, however, a body of princes who attain their titles only by dint of hard work, and executive capacity, coupled with life-long aspirations to devote themselves to the service of God. Contrary to the role of prince which comes to the sons of kings at birth, the Princes of the Roman Catholic Church must show by their native dignity, by their activities, their scholarship, and their self-sacrifice in the interests of God's work, that they are worthy and prepared to become one of the Sacred College of Cardinals. The Princes of the Roman Catholic Church are for the most part men of this mold.

Such a one was Cardinal Hayes. Princedom brought with it no change in the simplicity of the man. The aristocratic title signified in him nothing of the man who has achieved a sinecure for the rest of his life. It did not disturb the happy and simple

Irish qualities for which he had become loved by millions in the world's metropolis and in the highways and byways of the world leading to it. Neither did princedom relieve him of his daily routine of work and responsibility. Rather it intensified these, if the work attached to his archbishopric in the world's largest diocese could possibly have been intensified. Already he had been assuming great burdens, relatively localized to the immediate administration of his flock in the New York area. Also, from the time of the War he had been in charge of the Diocesis Castrensis, while exercising his duties as the Roman Catholic Chaplain-Bishop of America's armed forces.

As member of the Sacred College of Cardinals his duties called him into personal service of the Pope, as a Senator of the Church, and as an adviser in the privy council. The College of Cardinals to which he had been elevated is a unique body in the world's legislative institutions. It is a corporation, just as most amalgamations of companies are corporations, governed by corporation law. Its members are seventy, chosen from all countries with at least one from each country. Its divisions include three distinctions of rank, Cardinal-Bishops, Cardinal-Priests and Cardinal-Deacons. They alone have the right to elect the Pope; they are the Pope's counsellors in all important matters, matters embracing in their breadth diplomatic relations between the Vatican and the nations of every continent.

The Sacred College has been in active existence since the pontifical reign of Alexander III (1159-1181). It has remained to the present time a board of directors of Canon Law, each member required to give exact knowledge of all details relative to Canon Law, as well as to statutory relations between the Church and the State in his respective country. It shows the catholicity of the Roman Catholic Church in giving all citizens the opportunity to achieve this position of aristocratic elevation in the Church, which is a democracy of aristocrats. Even a layman is eligible to appointment as a member of the College of Cardinals.

Bishop Stephen J. Donahue, his Auxiliary Bishop and most intimate companion for years, testifies, with other personal friends, to the fact that it was Patrick Joseph Hayes' most sacred aspiration through the years of his boyhood and young manhood to become a priest; further than that aspiration, as we have said before, he had no ambition in this life. Bishop Donahue's words are these: "As a young man going to school and college, many an afternoon he spent in the presence of the Blessed Sacrament, pouring out the depths of his soul in prayer and petition that one day, if it was God's Holy Will, he might stand at the Altar of the Great High Priest. During the days of his sacerdotal ministry, his spiritual life was intimately bound up with the duties which were assigned to him by his superiors. In the days of his episcopate, his love for things spiritual grew more and more Christlike."

The Cardinal, we noted, accepted the Divine invitation to princedom humbly. It had meant everything in the world to him to be the recipient of Holy Orders which gave him the supreme power to bring God down from Heaven, and to place Him bodily on the tongues of thousands who knelt in humble pleading that Christ might share His life with him.

Out of millions whom the Master could have appointed to counsel His Vicar on earth, the boy whom the Egans long ago had envisioned in priestly vestment offering the Host on high, received the call to take his place among the few. He was ready and equipped when the call came. His superiors early had seen in him the intellect which would one day promote the Church still further in her traditional role of Mother of culture and progress as well as of spirituality. His post-Ordination work at the Catholic University singled him out among the students there doing research work, participating in seminars, composing theses and dissertations on advanced philosophical subjects. On completion of his studies, and while he was yet Chancellor under Cardinal Farley, he brought the hopes of his professors to realization when he began writing articles for the *North American Review* and also erudite contributions for the Catholic Encyclopedia. He was recognized even then as an authority on the new Marriage Law of the Church.

Thus when he was raised to the positions of

Bishop, Archbishop, and finally of Cardinal, he saw his promotion, not as the chance to exercise the new authority which each brought him, but as the opportunity, direct from God's hand, whereby he would have wider scope in performing his work as a priest. He always held close to his heart the revered truth that he was eternally a priest; the higher ranks of ecclesiastical offices were but the opening of doors leading him into places where the same sacerdotal work was to be continued, the only difference being that the phases of the work were now multiplied, the responsibilities heavier.

On the other hand, he knew that as Cardinal he would be attached directly to the Personal Representative of Christ on earth in the world senate, the privy council whose privilege it is to say who may be the Vicar and Representative of Christ. Moreover, the apostolic work of the priesthood, having taken on greater proportions, and having broadened his contacts, made him valuable in a personal way to the Holy Father as a consultant, and in the carrying out of Papal pronouncements in the Cardinal's own diocese three thousand miles removed from the Vatican.

As Prince he lost none of his geniality. New robes and opulent jewels to a lesser man than Patrick Cardinal Hayes might have spelled disastrous increase of the sense of his own importance. But this man took it all with a sort of dignified humor, a humor which was symbolic of his own nature. For he had never dreamed of himself as one day becoming a personage of prominence. The seriousness of his elevation he realized full well. He knew he would need added strength and perspicacity to meet the requirements of the role.

For these gifts he went to the same Source that had given him the fulfillment of his boyish wish— the priesthood. He made himself more humble than ever, and a more devoted son of his Blessed Mother. He took her as the inspiration of every success he had ever achieved. She was not a mere name, some far-away creature of power whom he had been told would prove valuable in life. She was his spiritual Mother, just as she is every man's spiritual Mother, but she was also an intimate love, the Lady Love and Queen Mother of his life, who never failed him. Bishop Donahue describes his devotion to her and the place of importance she held in his life:

"The Cardinal's devotion to the Blessed Mother of God was beautiful and tender in its simplicity. The loss of his own mother early in life increased his filial affection for her who knew the greatest of sorrow in the loss of a Son. It was his custom after the noon repast to pay a visit to the Blessed Sacrament. On these occasions he would lay a fresh-cut flower, which he carried from his table, at the feet of a statue of his Heavenly Queen.

"During the weeks of his summer vacation, he never failed every afternoon to visit the beautiful grotto of Our Lady of the Wayside, erected in the

hills at St. Joseph's in Monticello, New York. There
he would ask her protection for himself and his
diocese. The outstanding events of his priestly life
were in some way associated with the Mother of
God. He was baptized on the feast of her Presentation; was ordained on the feast of her Nativity; was
created a Cardinal on the eve of her Annunciation,
and was assigned the Church of Santa Maria in Via
as his Titular Church in Rome."

It was significant that he passed his last day at
St. Joseph's, Monticello, where the expression of his
love of the Blessed Mother may still be seen in the
Our Lady of the Wayside Grotto which he had built
to her honor. This little grotto, without the archi-
tectural trimmings which his Cardinal's Church in
Rome had, reflects the simplicity of the man's devotion. The latter was deep, and indescribable because
of its mystical nature. That little grotto meant as
much to him as did his Titular Roman edifice.

Many sought his advice and help. He himself
never decided on any matter, even of the smallest
detail, without consulting his divine Superior. Authority was his to exercise, but he knelt before the
Source of all authority in supplication for wisdom
and integrity in all things. The spirit of Americanism lived within him and was coincident with his
Catholicism. After the solemn ceremony which gave
him his elevation, his first utterance carried with it
his complete submission to the will of God, his eternal Superior. Who had chosen him, he knew, not

to be a figure of mere public prominence, but as a disciple whose life was to be continued in the more extended service of God. He knew that any honor that had come to him had come from Christ, the invisible Citizen of the world, and therefore, in his new role of Papal adviser, he was happier than ever before to be an American.

He was an American given a title in which might be considered by some a foreign royalty, in the sense that the Vatican lies in a foreign country. It was a tribute not only to Cardinal Hayes but also to America and the American people that one of their number was to take his place in such a corporation as the Sacred College of Cardinals. Immediately he set upon the continuation of the progressive work of the Church.

But he needed help, and naturally he implored the doctors of the Church. "The prayers of St. Augustine" (Bishop Donahue tells us) "that great Doctor of the Church, were constantly on his lips. He knew them from memory, and delighted to recite them aloud in his room while dressing and preparing for Mass '*Noverim Te, noverim me!*—That I might know Thee; that I might know myself,' was his daily morning offering. A spirit of prayer motivated every decision and act of his administration. The weighty problems and difficulties of his high office, after hours of work and prayer, were always laid at the throne of God with a confident hope that a satisfactory solution of them would be found. Without Christ his King he knew he could do nothing."

In the true spirit of the Catholic who asks intercession at the throne of God through the great army of saints, Cardinal Hayes sought help. He had, says Bishop Donahue, "a special devotion to St. John Chrysostom and St. Raphael the Archangel. To St. John Chrysostom he prayed daily asking for the grace to be able to preach the Gospel of Christ to his people in language that they would understand. Through St. Raphael he petitioned for the necessary health and strength to carry on the burden of his exalted office. . . As he was approaching the declining years of his life, the loving voice of Christ: 'Unless ye be converted and become as little children, ye cannot enter the kingdom of Heaven,' must have sounded constantly in his ears. Each day was consecrated to the service of his Master. Everything was done for Him, by Him, and with Him. The celebration of his daily Mass manifested a real act of faith and love in the ever Adorable Sacrament of the Eucharist."

His office called for action which would have effect in various parts of the world. It would seem that his divine Counsel Who gave him his promotion had been preparing him for these duties for some little while. His duties from the day he was ordained till the day he died were ever increasing; he was never known to consciously shirk one of them. The fact that as soon as one duty was completed another rose demanding attention, disturbed him not at all. For wherever Christ's work was being done there was an evidence of the spirit of Christ and the love of His followers for Him. Their contributions manifested Him. Their success proved His aid and His gratitude.

He never ceased showing his gratitude to God for the opportunity of being among the six Americans ever chosen to the Cardinalate. His aristocratic prestige took nothing away from his innate consciousness that he was also a democrat privileged to live in a democracy, though he often laughed as he remarked that his Celtic forbears might have been reluctant to be called prince because of their intense love of democracy!

Cardinal Hayes was a Prince of the Church, of men, of priests, and of charity.

Democracy is joyous in a son
Who walks a prince in crimson splendor clad,
But heavy lies the ermine on his heart
Who trod Manhattan's ways a lowly lad.

Can thrill be in a royal robe for him
Whose daily word his God has long obeyed?
Or would he seek the mountain solitudes
As He Who fled from earthly rule, afraid?

Meek Christ! Who wore a Cardinal's martyr red
Before the march that conquered Calvary,
His chalice take away, nor let him drink
This hour the draught of his Gethsemane!

CHAPTER X

CROSSES OF STRAW

IN the year 1921 I was with the Cardinal in mid-ocean, bound for the Holy City. After a dinner, in which restrained mirth was the order of the early evening, His Grace invited me to take a stroll with him on deck. The great ship was cleaving its rhythmic way majestically through the moonlit waters. The stars twinkled in the blue-black void above us. We were chatting about inconsequential personal experiences. There was no need for any confessional on my part. Patrick Joseph Hayes had been for nearly twenty years in a position to study the temperamental and spiritual weaknesses of his scholastic protégés.

We went on freely to a discussion of what were really crosses in our separate concepts. He expressed his sorrow that, in spite of the dominance of virtue in mankind as a whole, there should be so many victims of weakness brought to light when under fire as campaigners of the Church Militant. He intimated the sorrow in his own heart when he was made aware of challenges openly placed before Christ, not only by those without religious affiliation, but by His own spiritual subjects who had said truly, in the days of their innocence, "I live

now; yet not I, but Christ liveth in me," echoing
St. Paul, the mystic and apostle in sustained service
of his God. He expressed his hope that Christ's loyalists might ever grow stronger in their emulation of
St. Michael the Archangel, their safeguard against
the malice and snares of the devil. He referred to
the crosses of wood inherited by those worthy to be
designated 'other Christs' as relatively easy to be
borne by the latter with divine assistance. He la-
mented the readiness of national or racial groups to
respond to the impulse that brings men into the role
of Herod slaughtering the innocents—the children
who are war's most pathetic victims. He could hear
his divine Master weeping as He said, "When ye did
it unto the least of these, my little ones, ye did it
unto Me!" He found a heavy cross of wood in war's
price for so-called glory. His heart's grief was expressed in the words of his invocation: "O, almighty
and loving Father, in Whom we live, move, and
have our being; without Whom we can do nothing;
and to know Whom is to live; and to serve Whom is
to reign; do Thou, we humbly beseech Thee, pour
out abundantly the unction of Thy heavenly benediction upon our beloved country, especially in this
direful hour of world history, that America may
neither do nor suffer evil, but continue to enjoy
Thy all-powerful protection and Thy all-bounteous
favor!" This was his plea that he be given divine
assistance in bearing his cross as the Alter Christus
on the Via Dolorosa.

He found the cross to be a wooden weight but also a source of happiness when he was Chaplain-Bishop. "O Father of might, wisdom, and justice, Who, by gracious ordinance has vested in nations the right of self-government, and in an all-loving Providence has brought into being our mighty and glorious Republic of more than one hundred millions of freemen, dedicated to political, social, and religious liberty, we pray Thee to make our beloved America the happiest of peoples, with the wisest rulers and the best of government, in order that all who dwell in our land may in every truth know and rightly value the priceless heritage of American freedom."

There was a load of sorrow pressing upon his heart as he studied the desolation of the many firesides left chill through the erring ways of the self-blinded who groped through life as the victims of bigotry. "The Church watches firmly over the home. The Church is the burning bush of Moses on holy ground, ever aflame with the fire of God, and never consumed. The Church is the fiery chariot of Elias, drawn by brilliant horses across the skies of the centuries ever in motion and ever in the eye of the world until the crack of doom."

There was no grief bearing more pitilessly upon his heart than that which was his as he pondered the plight of little children desolate and hungering for the bare necessities of life. "You cannot give employment and you cannot give money in this time of stress and trial. I think what we want of you is that you be cheerful and sunny and not bear the responsibilities of your elders. I think the Lord would be more moved by the prayers of you children than by the prayers of your elders."

He found a vivid sympathy with Christ, crowned with thorns, as he reflected upon the misery of children whose parents were indifferent to their soul's desire for contact with the Christ Child and the Man pleading for their nearness to Himself. "It is my privilege from time to time to meet prominent men in all sections of the United States, and frequently the question is asked of me: 'Do men in New York City go to church?' and I always tell them that five or six thousand policemen of the city of New York attend divine service, not merely in a passing way but that they receive Holy Communion. They throw up their hands and say, 'Thank God, America is safe.' And then I tell them that these policemen are simply a part of the great Catholic legion, all of whom acknowledge God, bend the knee, and are not ashamed to proclaim the fact that they believe in Christ and rejoice to be numbered among His followers."

He found his own limited physical resources to be a cross of wood when he was denied the stamina to respond to his own impulses of rescue in a broader field where humanity in trouble beckoned to his priestly heart. He found in his own helplessness a quiet consolation when he dwelt upon it in

meditation as the privilege of emulating Christ helpless on the Cross. It was in those three hours that
the Master of life did most—while helpless—for
helpless humanity. He was bowed with grief when
he beheld immortals stricken by their own parents'
indifference to the needs of offspring entrusted to
them or consenting to the slaughter of the unborn.
"Disastrous beyond possibility of description to society is the condition when women measure their
lives, not by the number of their offspring, but by
the number of their husbands. Pagan Rome at the
height of its imperial power, with a conquered
world paying tribute to the Caesars, sealed slowly
but surely its own doom. No foe without proved so
terrible an enemy as corruption within. Widespread
divorce desecrated the sanctuary of the family with
the consequent degradation of woman. The con-
structive forces of the empire were weakened by the
deadly moral poisons that Roman society absorbed
into its very vitals and took no means to throw off.
When this happens in the human body death follows."

In bearing these heavier crosses, the other
Christ found a peace in his heart that the world
cannot give, the peace that radiates from the Real
and Mystical Presence of Christ Who lives within
the élite called to his banquet board. And knowing
this, I found myself somewhat surprised and very
grateful when he revealed the humanity in his heart
by confiding to me the little annoyances encoun-

tered in life's journey. As we paced the deck, he grew more serious. Finally, as if with a sudden resolve to release the thought trembling on his lips, he called me to look out to sea as we rested upon the rail. "Father John," he said, "whenever you meet the prayer in the Mass, *'pro Antistiti nostro'*— (the prayer 'for our spiritual superior in the diocese') — please make your intention the one that means most to me as a personal gift. Beg Our Blessed Lord to give me the necessary grace to bear what Saint Augustine terms 'the crosses of straw.' It is the trifling annoyances of life, the proneness to impatience I find in my soul when I am approached by persons who will not accept anything but a spoken agreement with themselves, as they plead for selfish removal of a competitor so that they may advance to honors selfishly ambitioned and detrimental to the common good. They are the weepers at the wailing wall who present their peevish protests against humanity in general which fails to recognize their imagined talents. They are self-made martyrs who are a source of unrest to all who come within the radius of their unfortunate personalities. Please ask Our Blessed Lord to give me the supreme strength, through divine grace, to restrain impulses to tell each of them my heart's tendency to disdain their presence!"

This quiet, but nonetheless intense, plea of the man who was to all of his intimates a symbol of serenity was a revelation to me. I was grateful to find the temptation to intolerance of human nuisances even in the saint of my boyhood and its ensuing years. I promised with a full heart conscientiously to heed his request, and since his departure I have offered a prayer to him daily, asking that he plead with the Powers above that I may at least be given the grace to make a beginning in an attempt to attain the same aspiration, so much more distant from me than from him.

And I am sure that his departed spirit is watching over all of us on this earth.

Prayer for a Bishop

Lift not, dear Lord, the Cross of Wood from him
 Who cherishes as Thou the heavy beams
That spread Thy royal couch on Calvary,
 When Thou didst lay Thee down to triumph's
  dreams.

Nor take the Cross of Gold that marks his breast,
 The sign of David's Son to priesthood born,
Whose high command e'en Thou shalt deign to
  serve
 As suns obey Thy call at eve and morn.

But be Thou his Cyrenean, dear Lord,
 When he is called the leaden load to draw
Of cares that seem too slight for sacrifice:
 Lend him Thy strength to bear each Cross of
  Straw.

CHAPTER XI

Ad Evitandum Cardinalatum

AS I walked through the shadows of a glimmering February dawn of 1921 in the Holy City of Rome few were the wayfarers treading the ancient lanes of history's banquet hall. My destination was St. Peter's Basilica where the sacristan of the edifice was waiting to assist me in preparing for the offering of the Holy Sacrifice of the Mass on the tomb of the Apostles Peter and Paul.

In my brief meditation before vesting for the celebration, thoughts crowded in upon me suggesting a choice of intentions to be placed before the Giver of all gifts when offering the Son to the Father in the Holy City's Holy of Holies. It was quite natural for me to revert in thought to the kindly gentleman whose courtesy of invitation had made the offering of the Mass in the Eternal City's sanctuary a blessed opportunity for myself. A few weeks back I had found on my desk in New York a letter bearing the address of his residence, and the script so familiar to those with whom he corresponded. Opening the missive with unrestrained haste, I read his summons to appear before him immediately to discuss a matter that might be of "mutual interest." I was immediately plunged into a whirl of conjectures as to possible reasons for the summons. Would it be his conscience prompting him to demand of me a report of stewardship in my role of spiritual director of the Catholic Big Brother activities in his archdiocese? Would it be the announcement of his decision to assign me as chaplain to some institution of education or correction during my convalescence from the physical disorder from which I was then suffering? Could he have heard about some of the comments I was prone to utter after missing a three-foot putt needed for a half?

Dressed in my everyday best I appeared before him on the day and hour designated. Without any time-wasting preliminaries he told me that he had decided to embark from the port of New York on a trip to Italy.

"I am leaving on January twelfth of the year that is now upon us," he told me. "Knowing that it is your birthday, I have decided to celebrate it on a seagoing vessel departing on the same day. So get ready for the big adventure! I have already arranged, with the assistance of Monsignor Dineen and Dr. Donahue, your transportation needs. Monsignor Arcese of Monticello, New York, will complete the party."

His announcement of the good time in prospect left me all but dumb with gratitude. After my mumbled "Thank you, Your Grace!" he went on to say that he would like to attend to all the expenses of travel for the party and that he would be easier of mind if he were assured that I had the necessary pocket money "for smokes and the like." He handed me an envelope which he told me to open on arrival in my living quarters.

After receiving his blessing and making the usual gesture of obedience and loyalty to all that his episcopal ring suggested in authority, I made for the stairway and exit on the floor below. A sincere attempt to convince myself that my heart was reasonably indifferent as to what might be in the envelope he had given me proved ineffective and I opened the unsealed depository to find a check for one thousand dollars and his card bearing the inscription "For cigarettes. P. J. H." The combination of invitation to be one of his party, and also of being endowed with more than enough to play the role of peer and leisurely globe-trotter, made me feel like a masculine edition of Cinderella planning her attire for the big scene at the ball. I learned afterwards that he had made his bequest so magnificent because he felt that I might have outstanding accounts to be met, incurred by my recent visit to physicians for advice and treatment.

The trip abroad was made all the more delightful as a holiday excursion by the presence of Monsignor Joseph P. Dineen, Doctor Stephen J. Donahue, the prelate's second secretary, and Monsignor Vincenzo Arcese, the old friend of the prelate who has through the years of their priesthood been his intimate and host in St. Joseph's, Monticello, New

York. It was in this happy retreat that the priest and official found the recuperative factors necessary for him to meet his multiplied obligations of soul and ecclesiastical assignments.

The intervening days before the date of departure were a mingling of preparations for the trip with the most impressive figure on my personal horizon, and of anticipations that were all-absorbing dreams of big things to come. I found myself utterly incapable of acting as if it were just one of the exceptionally happy gifts that an indulgent Providence had contributed to my days up to that time. And there was not the slightest incident in the realization of anticipated joys that did not justify my irrepressible eagerness for the adventure. Being tolerated by the group that made up the Archbishop's official family was in itself an achievement. But I also found myself encouraged by my host to join in the lively discussions at meals. I was accorded my turn in being called by him to pace the decks of the liner in his morning strolls. He was just as ready to discuss the events in the different sports arenas as he was to invite an exchange of ideas on the personal joys to be found in exercising the prerogatives of our common priesthood. He would mingle on occasions with groups of our fellow passengers, exchanging anecdotes that had many a laugh in them.

Offering Mass on shipboard was a privilege we all enjoyed owing to his prestige in obtaining the necessary permission for us. It was always an opportunity appreciated by angels to be present when he offered the Holy Sacrifice at any altar. He radiated a vibrant contentment of soul as he went through the simple ceremonies of the sacrificial rite. His movements were as quietly graceful as his eyes were contemplative. He was lost in thoughts of Christ, Whose divine powers he was privileged to exercise as the Alter Christus, but he was at the same time observing the smallest demands of the order of the ritual.

Arriving in Rome after disembarking in Naples, we found a hearty welcome extended by Monsignor Charles O'Hern, of happy memory, the Rector of the American College situated in the Holy City. The Vice-Rector, Doctor Bernard J. Mahoney, now Bishop of Sioux Falls, South Dakota, was a generous factor in making the party comfortable in the somewhat ancient institution that housed the American aspirants to the priesthood of Christ. His kindly Irish-American heart was bent upon giving his guests as many of the comforts of home as are reasonably available in lands across the sea.

While the Archbishop and his devoted secretaries were going about their official business I found opportunity to wander about Rome at will. Saint Peter's with its memories of history-making events was a sacramental suggestive of Christ perpetuated in His pontiffs. Even to a person of my own all too-limited knowledge of history's highlights, there were stories on all sides that pulsed with drama. The chance to study art's progress in the Vatican galleries is a rich one, and I was permitted to ramble at will along the walls that held aloft the masterpieces of geniuses, and revealed the beginnings offered by Cimabue, Giotto, the pre-Raphaelites, and the masters whose works were created in succeeding ages. Andrea del Sarto is to me the supreme genius of art's history, his works challenging detection of line in his masterpieces that are a liquid blend of one color tone into another. It was perhaps this absorption in the masters departed that prompted me to seek and to find an artist looked upon as a worthy offspring of the Renaissance masters, one who would paint a portrait of New York's Archbishop which would be worthy of his character and rank.

Having found an artist willing and capable of undertaking this commission, I requested my host to put aside three half-hour periods to be given the artist for the creation of a souvenir and memento of the current trip and our visit to the Holy City. His reaction to the proposal was as immediate as it was uncompromising. "Father John!" he said in firm tones, accompanied by gesture of the hand suggesting a grateful but definite refusal of the proffered gift, "I must insist that you do absolutely nothing in souvenir investments. This party is all my own, and I will share with none the host's role! Please omit flowers!" Knowing that his tone indicated his adamant decision I bowed to his will. He would have been equally determined if I had bought an original manuscript of the early illuminators in monastic studies, or a set of vestments or some like souvenir precious to one of his cultured taste.

The means of registering my gratitude to him was my constant problem in those memorable days abroad. In spite of his very sincere protests I found it all but impossible to refrain from picking up something in the way of a local memento that would indicate my sense of appreciation. It may readily have been a suggestion from above that finally led me to do the right thing in his eyes. I found a real friend in the sacristan of St. Peter's Basilica. Through this kindly gentleman I obtained permission to celebrate Holy Mass on the altar above the tomb of Saints Peter and Paul. It was necessary for me to arrive early in order to finish the service before the arrival of visiting dignitaries, the first of whom would begin his Mass at seven on the morning assigned to me.

Arriving in the sacristy at six o'clock I took a little time for a pre-Mass meditation. I pleaded with the divine Friend of us all to suggest the best way for me to show a semblance of gratitude to Himself as well as to the Archbishop, for the countless favors and blessings in return for which I had never yet been able to find a way of evincing my heart's thanks. I was prompted to attempt an expression of gratitude by offering up the Holy Sacrifice of the Mass for the intention which His devotee Patrick

Joseph Hayes had confided to his Master as the dominant desire then in his heart.

But as I went on in my necessarily hurried attempt at recollection, my thoughts turned to interests that had captured my attention in the past few days. Here and there I had heard comments of the Archbishop's being not only eligible but desirable as a member of the College of Cardinals. These expressions of opinion did not emanate from men given to the role of prophets self-sufficiently announcing coming events over which they had no control. They were persons in a position to, and of a disposition to give utterance only to opinions based on logical inference. Each time I heard their passing remarks I was more inclined to ponder the reaction upon the Archbishop should there be a realization of these honors. I knew that he would have nothing but the sincerest appreciation of the proffered honor. He was vividly conscious of the privilege that would be his were he called into the élite group who made up the Sacred College. Its members are the personal selection of the Holy Father seeking advisers in the administration of his holy vocation.

Nevertheless I was unable to eliminate from my thoughts the fear that the functions, canonical and sacred, traditionally associated with the routine of the candidate called to membership in the Papal Senate, might have a regrettable reaction on the Archbishop's health were he called to meet them at that time. Then came the fear that I might be necessarily dramatizing for myself the scene pending. I might easily be falling into the weakness of wanting to be "different." But I felt an urge, which I hoped was holy, to request the Master and divine Exponent of common sense to postpone the designation of my good friend and mentor to a later date, when he would be in more robust health and under less pressure of obligations than at the moment. Whatever may have been the psychological process, or spiritual inspiration, I made my intention of the Mass offered that morning, the plea that he would be spared the call to a seat in the College of Cardinals until a later period of his life.

After the celebration of the Holy Sacrifice and a period spent in thanksgiving, I found myself incapable of regret that I had offered the Mass for the intention determined upon. I returned to the American College, made my way to the Archbishop's rooms at about eight o'clock, and was permitted to chat with him for a while.

Without undue preliminaries I said, "Your Grace! I found a present for you this morning!"

He received my timid, if eager, announcement with a characteristic calm that made me feel that he was studying a case interesting because of its oddity. "Well, you will have your own way!" he remarked, somewhat resignedly. "Get the present out and give it to me so that I may express my thanks appropriately."

"Your Grace," I said, "there is nothing tangible to get out in the way of an offering. I just wish to tell you that I offered Mass today on the altar of the tomb of Saints Peter and Paul—I offered the Mass as a prayer for your spiritual and physical welfare." His eyes beamed their genuine appreciation of the gift. "I'll tell you the *exact* intention in my own heart when I was offering the Holy Sacrifice if you'll promise not to suspend me on hearing it."

He looked at me with eyes that suggested his bewilderment in hearing my statement. After a moment of thought he replied, "I will certainly make no such promise to you. You'll either freely tell me or keep the matter a secret entirely your own!"

Then I found the courage to say, "Nothing ventured, nothing gained! So here goes! I asked Our Blessed Lord to postpone your designation as a Cardinal to a later date—to a time when you'll be in better condition to accept the honor!"

At this announcement he evinced a surprise mingled with unmistakable gravity, indicating—to me, at least—a friend shocked. In something like brooding mystification, he paced back and forth in the room for a time. "Father John!" he said, "I hope that you are not inclined to be facetious in referring to your intention at the Holy Sacrifice of the Mass?" I immediately stated that I had never been more reverently serious in my life. This caused him to pace the room again, silently absorbed in thoughts that gave him the appearance of a man at a loss to frame words expressive of his mystification. I had, in the meantime, come to the conclusion that I had hurt the deepest sensibilities of a very dear friend. He was convinced, I concluded, that I had confided to the divine Friend of us all the conscientious conviction in my impulsive soul that he was not of the fiber that Princes of the Church are made of. I was embarrassed in the conviction that I had hurt the man who was in truth to all of his friends another Christ as far as his wholehearted offer of self would permit his living the ideal.

After two or three minutes of silence he went to a desk in the room, unlocked it and drew forth a little book. Turning to me he said, "Father John! I am about to show you a little inscription that I had thought would never be read by eyes other than my own! . . . I am impelled to show it to you because of the striking coincidence to be found in it. We have never exchanged a syllable in our many conversations that touched on the subject of ecclesiastical advancement and official recognition. The coincidence involved in the subject at hand is too striking to keep the secret from you." With these words he hesitatingly placed the page before me. There I saw written under the current date his own Mass intention, phrased in the words, *"Ad evitandum Cardinalatum!"*

For those of my readers who may not be familiar with the Latin, I may say that he had gone before his divine Master that morning at the altar and had prayed that He, the King of Kings, would avert from his unworthy self the call to membership in the College of Cardinals, the body of men who are the Princes of the universal Church.

One of those to whom I confided this occurrence, on my return, was Father Duffy, the priest, scholar, and militant of immortal memory. His immediate reaction prompted him to advise me to keep the incident a secret as long as the Cardinal remained in our midst. "That episode," said Father Duffy prophetically, "will do more than a book specializing on the sanctity of his character! When a man appears before God, at the altar upon which he is offering the Eucharistic Sacrifice, there pleading with the Source of all honors worth the gaining, to withhold the gift that is second in ecclesiastical dignity only to the Papacy, he is revealing the humility of Christ Who 'fled into a high mountain, Himself alone, lest they make Him king.'"

CHAPTER XII

Cardinal Hayes, the Saint

IN applying to Cardinal Hayes the title "saint," I am aware that many readers, wholeheartedly devoted to our departed prelate, may find themselves inclined to pity the devotion of a zealot to a friend. The Church has ever pursued the technique of the research scholar before arriving at the point where she feels satisfied in the important decision of canonization. Aware that this designation has all the earmarks of special pleading, it is a challenge to the fair-minded and sympathetic to express an opinion as to what constitutes sanctity in a soul. I honestly believe that mine is a verdict that comes, not from overplayed sentimentality, but from a sincere survey of the career, acts, words, devoutness, and humility of one who lived his every hour within the shadow of Christ's Cross; of one who was never able to keep out of his waking thoughts the fascination of Christ.

While we think of him as a saint, the picture of Cardinal Hayes the saint is not an image of some brooding man of dim ages past, with downcast eyes and clasped hands, moving about in a wilderness, isolated, aloof, disdainful of the world, its problems, and evils. True sainthood is a flesh and blood product in which are the qualities of mind and heart which spur men and women on to sustained action in the name of Christ. Saints make enemies as well as friends, even as Christ foretold when He said to His future Apostles, "The world will hate you."

It is no worthy boast to say that one has not made enemies in all his years. A saint is a hero who has conquered those forces of the universe which, in their softness and voluptuousness, have thrown their strength against him to keep him from finding the Grail, the trophy of victory. It must be won by him alone in the darkness of night and in the brilliance of day. And in his victory his name is seldom heralded in the texts of history.

Patrick Cardinal Hayes was himself an instance of the inspiration to joy that is in the heart of all who walk with Christ. In the homely poorness of his youth he had developed the richness of simplicity. It lay in quiet fun, and grew to a mature sense of healthy cheerfulness, ripening out of his belief in Christ's message that the world was made by Him a place for human beings to exult in the creation of all things. Life and the world were the happy valley for the voyager with Christ, rather than a pilgrimage through a "vale of tears."

His garb of priesthood did not imply for him the doffing of the happy mood. It was happiness to fast, to meditate, to pray, to offer daily acts of self-sacrifice—all in gratitude for the gifts of God. He always referred to Christ as "The Master" and the success of life as he summed it up for himself was the serving of Christ, Who is Sanctity Incarnate. *"Noverim Te, noverim me*—Let me know Thee, that I may know myself." This was the Cardinal's morning offering.

The saint sees work to be done and does it. It is not the mere seeing that makes him a saint. It is the doing. Christ was the youthful Doer; not the brooder. His popularity among the Jews proved this. They marveled at His actions, His words; above all, at His courageous stand for justice in the face of the political force wielded by temporal rulers and Pharisees. The Jewish masses who followed Him were so enthusiastic about Him that they would have had Him as their temporal ruler. Nowhere else had they seen or heard of one like Him, for He took chances with His citizenship by mingling with social outcasts. No one else in His time had talked publicly with or befriended sinners, lepers, beggars, the blind, and lame. It was amazing to them to hear His ready wit in such instant retorts as, "Render unto Caesar the things that are Caesar's, and unto God the things that are God's." The poor were His constant care and source of solicitude.

Patrick Cardinal Hayes was a twentieth-century imitator of Christ, the Saviour of the World, "Whose majestic stature, Divine teaching, and inspiring example live on through all the centuries that were, that are, and that ever can be. His is the way, the truth, and the life, that mark and bless with surety, safety, and happiness the pathway of human progress, both in time and eternity." In these words, His disciple presented one of many portraits of his Master.

Idealistic educators these days talk and write of the impertinence of establishing leaders who have the interests of the people at heart. "To make the world a safer place to live in" has become the catchword of ambitious politicians and statesmen. Children in the schools are taught the deeds of presidents, kings, dictators, conquerers. Cardinal Hayes was taught the chivalry of national heroes when he was a lad, but the Hero he chose will remain ever sovereign and eternally invincible. "The sovereignty of Christ over the world which He has redeemed," said His Eminence, "should be unreservedly acknowledged, with all its implications, by a Christian people and a Christian civilization. Failure to do so upsets radically the equilibrium of the moral, social, and religious world."

The primacy of Christ he held above all things. "The supreme, absolute and universal empire of Christ over all things created, visible and invisible, especially over the mind, the will, and the heart of man, does not permit the division some would make that would exclude Christ and His principles from the ordinary, daily life of mankind."

A man living this creed is undeniably a saint in the making. In a world of turmoil, he played the part of the militant, fighting for righteousness. In the achievement of his tasks he won the admiration of millions; he won also the opposition of some, even as Christ won bitter enmity in going about His Father's business. As priest, Bishop, Archbishop, Chaplain, Cardinal, he was the doer, inserting himself in the affairs of men in the interest of men. His enterprises furthered social and economic happiness, for they were based on a spiritual premise: the religious education of youth shapes the character of the adult; the destiny of the state hinges on the success of that training. "The child is father to the man." The inner peace, intelligence, wisdom of men and women can be gained only by the subjection of the will to the eternal verities taught by Christ and perpetuated by His Popes, His clergy and the army of men who live the Commandments of God.

Cardinal Hayes once said: "From the valley below the mountain, among minds 'tossed to and fro and carried about with every wind of doctrine' (Ephesians IV, 14), there roll up unceasingly against the Rock clouds of ignorance, bigotry, hatred, and calumny, only to be dissipated as empty vapor in the sunlight of Divine Truth. 'Kings of the earth have stood up and princes met together' (Psalms II, 2), with unsheathed sword to rage furiously in vain against the immovable Rock of Peter."

Here is the conflict of man, looking for peace in the conquest of man. But to the Cardinal in Manhattan, the essence of peace came from the sense of stability cemented by the unity of the millions who claim membership in the dynasty of Rome. For this is the dynasty of eternal peace. To keep that unity inviolable required constant conflict with the forces seeking to undermine it. Into the lists he rode, armed with the wisdom of the Church, her doctrine, her tradition, her fathers' philosophy and, above all, the miraculous substantiation of the teachings of her Founder.

Few men of like prominence had as few opponents and critics as the Cardinal. But he entered the battle against the army of Error—pragmatism, birth control, indecency on the stage and screen, loose tendencies by some of the press, obscene magazines, suggestive advertising displays, child labor, fortuitous legislation, evils brought by the depression, the human tendency to despair under adverse conditions, the World War and its ensuing breakdown of the gates of restraint. Each of these constitutes a separate problem luring human society away from the life of the soul. Progress might have ceased had not prelates recognized the doom that faced mankind. Cardinal Hayes, resplendent in his robes of clerical dignity, might himself have chosen the easiest way to popular acclaim by going along uttering platitudes about the harsh realities of life. But he didn't. He literally challenged every malign influence. He fought a personal public duel with each of them when his conscience prompted him to meet the challenge.

Courage was his mainstay—courage, faith, prayer, and a dynamic urge to the Church with its immeasurable wellsprings of life, peace, decency, happiness. He did not attempt to fight hatred with hatred, force with force. Tolerance was the bulwark of his defense. Sanctity was his chosen ally. One can scarcely call it a weapon for it was not used by him as a flashing sword. In his hands it was not a scourge but an unction. Those who knew him intimately and worked with him in the personal contact of routine activities have testified to his childlike characteristics, notably love and benevolence. In his chiding he never lashed out. Rather, his appeal to the inherent goodness of people was an appeal to men's intelligence, faith, optimism and their sense of right.

When he ascended the pulpit to repudiate immoral and unmoral acts and institutions, he presented his thesis point for point in well-ordered emphasis. His life was a constant study, enhanced by daily acknowledgment, before the Blessed Sacrament, of his own unworthiness. No man working alone against the forces he set himself against could have been capable of the success that came to him. His success came from the womb of the Blessed Mother to whom he never ceased to pray. The Holy Trinity listened to his plea impressed on his coat of arms: *"Mane Nobiscum, Domine!"*

He rose each morning at four o'clock and for an hour prayed and meditated before the Blessed Sacrament in the chapel at his residence. The milkman returning from his deliveries, the policeman on his solitary beat, the taxicab men cruising along the city's streets, the busmen on their early schedules, the millions yet asleep in lowly apartments,—all were included in his prayers. He besought Christ that the grace of God might shine through each soul in his archdiocese. He besought peace for the nations of men; not vast territories or riches for the individual aspirant. Peace, happiness, joy, fun, righteousness, good living, honesty, the love of neighbor for neighbor, charity—these he knew to be the real needs of the world and he asked that the world be granted these to share.

In his meditation he usually maintained a seated posture, occasionally reading from the works of one of the Fathers of the Church. At seven forty-five he offered the Holy Sacrifice of the Mass, after which he continued his contemplation and offered his thanksgiving. At nine o'clock he broke his fast, enjoying breakfast with his secretary and his chancellor who lived with him. A visit to the Blessed Sacrament followed breakfast and then he gave himself over to executive business until one o'clock.

After dinner the Cardinal again spent some time in the chapel, where he communed with his Divine Master. His custom during these after dinner visitations was, as we have seen, to leave a bouquet of flowers at the foot of the Blessed Virgin's statue, his daily tribute and gift to the Lady he loved.

Before continuing his business of the day, he would have a half-hour's afternoon nap, after which he repaired to his desk or appeared at whatever function happened to be on his schedule for the day. Cardinal Hayes' popularity rose to such an extent during his public career that it became humanly impossible for a man to respond to one-tenth of the invitations sent him.

One hour preceding his evening meal he spent in adoration. At this time he held in his hands a crucifix, pondering on the sorrowful mysteries of the Divine Victim. In his room at nine o'clock he remained cloistered, praying and reading from the works of the Church Fathers. St. Augustine and St. Thomas Aquinas he knew by heart. This hour, following his adoration, was a period during which he tolerated no interruption. The philosophy and theology of the Fathers were his sacred readings, his daily review of the doctrine which gave him his authority in the senate of the Church. While vesting himself for Mass in the morning, he would repeat excerpts from these readings.

The philosophies expounded by St. Augustine and St. Thomas lived in his mind through all his later years, even as they had been uppermost in his consciousness during his seminary days when he and Father Duffy used to discuss precepts of the Church and the theology on which they were founded.

Each night he said his Rosary, offering each Hail Mary in an earnest request that he might administer the affairs of his See wisely, sincerely, effectively. Just before retiring he murmured his last prayer, to the Archangel Raphael whom he trusted to remain at his side as his guardian while he slept. This was his invocation to Our Lord, which he never failed to recite at least once a day:

"Mane Nobiscum Domine!"

"Stay with us, Lord! Stay with me in my new and heavy duties, in my responsibilities, my solicitudes, my fatigues, my anxieties, my sorrows borne for my people! Stay with me, Lord, for if You stay I have sufficient help to carry me along to successful accomplishment for the extension of Your earthly Kingdom! Stay with me, O Lord, to direct and to govern all my aspirations, my impulses, my actions for Thy Greater Glory!"

Just before retiring he would kiss the hands and feet of the crucifix. His prayer to St. Joseph was: "St. Joseph, friend of the Sacred Heart of Jesus, pray for me."

CHAPTER XIII

"It Is Consummated."

WHEN the life of Patrick Cardinal Hayes is seen in retrospect there come to mind some of the Horatio Alger stories that held us fascinated when we were boys. When we study the scene of the prelate's birth, we contrast its utter simplicity with the splendor that attended his obsequies. It is the contrast between the birth and death scenes that frequently tells the degree of success in the lives of men and women considered great by their surviving contemporaries and posterity.

The future Cardinal's mother was a daughter of Erin, one of nature's self-effacing gentlewomen who lived in the presence of her God while a holy lilt was in her heart. She was frail in physique and went about her business quietly, expending herself in the fulfillment of domestic duties and the demands of her spiritual routine. When she was passing out of the realm of Time she made a will in the form of a whispered word to her Creator and Judge —the Eucharistic Presence within her bosom—asking Christ to pass on to her boy any virtues she might possess. The boy's father was still her ideal of romantic manhood, and she prayed that the lad's happy inheritance would be the loyalty of his father to all the revealed ideals of Christ. The Prince of the Church cherished many sacred memories of his all too few days with his parents.

There is a subtly touching intimation of his heart's reverence for his relatives, the Egans, when he spoke once of the Catholic Sisters of Charity: "I wonder how many women, how many mothers, would be willing to take the offspring of someone else to their bosom, a child abandoned to the streets of this great city, and love that child, and give it everything they have, that is their time, their life, their service night, noon, and morning, day after day, and year after year. That is what these Catholic Sisters of Charity have been doing for fifty years or more." In these words we sense his love of the noble Egan couple who took the place of the Sisters when he, himself, needed a Nazareth in which he could "advance in wisdom and age and grace with God and men."

Vivid reminiscences of his boyhood days and sacred influences were given utterance when he said, "I am overjoyed, as the Archbishop of this diocese, to find myself here rejoicing with the good Salesian Fathers and the people of the Transfiguration parish on the glorious occasion of the celebration of the centenary of this parish. . . It was the old parochial school here which it was my privilege to attend fifty years ago, when, as a boy, I lived in this neighborhood."

His reverence for the Christian Brothers, the

heroes of his boyhood, youth, manhood, and priest-hood, finds expression in his words suggesting the adventures he found in their presentation of the Church Militant. "The trails blazed by the Catholic missionaries through forest, atop mountains, across rivers, and over prairies have developed into tri-umphal highways along which Catholic faith has erected hundreds and hundreds of temples and tab-ernacles to our Eucharistic King."

Msgr. Fulton J. Sheen, in a radio address on October 5, 1938, expressed to the millions who ab-sorbed his trembling message, his heart's reverence for the saint of our day just called to be a guest of the Holy Family in the eternal Nazareth, when he said: "America has just lost the greatest man of this present generation—Patrick Cardinal Hayes!" He went on to tell of the prelate's early morning devo-tions and prolonged preparation for Mass which was always "offered with such unction and devotion. . . When he sat down before his desk after three and a half hours of spiritual and Sacramental communion with God you could walk before it and feel that you were in the presence of Christ."

The same simple desk that served his predeces-sors served him. His bedroom was only fourteen by sixteen without an attached bath, and except for the statue of Our Lady beside his bed, the Crucifix over it, and a few pictures on the wall, the room con-tained no furniture but an old bed and two old chairs. In the last few years of his life his physicians would not let him say his night prayers on his knees. Accordingly, he said them in bed with his head propped by three pillows, one of which he would remove on retiring. Alongside his bed was a glass of water and a small tablet which he would take after his night prayers just before he fell asleep. He turned out all the lights in his room as he prayed at night, but kept his hands folded across his breast, holding a Crucifix. As he lifted his soul to God he would run his fingers over the Cross and the image of the Crucified Saviour—"One needed no light to know that love was there."

That was the way he died—saying his night prayers. The water had not been touched, nor the tablet, nor the third pillow. Without any convulsions, he died as he prayed, and the next morning they found him as if asleep, with his hands folded across his breast, and his eyes looking down upon the Crucified Saviour. Thus died America's greatest citizen, and the Church's greatest priest.

And that is what Cardinal Hayes was above all things else—a priest, a member of all families, but belonging to none; living in the world, and yet not of it; serving the poor not as one giving, but as one receiving; lifting man to God in the Consecration and bringing God to man in the Communion; going to work from prayer and to prayer from work; being hard on himself and easy on others; hating sin but loving the sinner; being intolerant of falsehood, but tolerant to persons; being a priest to others, and a victim to Christ! What a vocation! That is the priesthood! That is Cardinal Hayes."

The scene is now laid in a temple that symbolizes in its very atmosphere the aspirations of the human soul to attain place in the realm of eternal rest and perpetual interest. Saint Patrick's Cathedral has been for the better part of a century the sanctuary of weary men and women seeking the peace which the world cannot give. On September 9, 1938, within its walls there was a throng whose grief-stricken hearts throbbed in unison before the silent figure whose remains were elevated and resting upon a catafalque in the center of the edifice. Cardinal Hayes lay there in solitary state, a symbol of the faith that achieves the great hope of all who are here in the vineyard of time awaiting the reward eternal of their labors of love. A profound silence met one's ears as one entered the Cathedral after having stepped aside from the din and clangor of New York's teeming streets. Men and women moved along the aisles with reverent, solemn tread.

The measured pealing of the elevated organ suggested the choirs of weeping angels who once sang their joy over Bethlehem, but who were screened from Calvary's sacrificial altar by the blackness that hung as a veil between heaven and earth when the Light of the world was quenched as He breathed out the last happy words of victory "It is consummated." The heavy silence, tremulous with the rich organ music, was an eloquent expression of the reverence begotten of faith.

The spirit of Patrick Cardinal Hayes was all but palpable to those who bowed their heads in contemplation during the sacred hour given to prayer for his soul in the Cathedral. The rich man was there meditating upon the wealth of peace which the departed priest had found in a life spent in the real and mystical presence of Christ. Men and women who had achieved places of eminence in empires of commerce extending over both hemispheres now turned their thoughts upon their own souls. Inwardly they sought for something approaching comparative success in the light of their friend's blessed possession of that contentment in this life which the world can neither give nor buy.

The remains of their friend resting in a Temple of God bade these sorrowing men and women turn their thoughts to the reality of an eternal future. Many of them had evaded the urgent plea their conscience had been whispering for years. They were good men, as the world judges goodness. But now they found it impossible to dismiss the insistent voice that was constantly reminding them of a life eternal for which the life in time is but a rehearsal. They had come to an age of life when preparedness for the last hour of life on earth was daily becoming more of a pressing necessity. They had found out that—as Monsignor Humphrey Moyniham has said—"the truly illustrious professors of the world have nothing but profound contempt for the materialism thrust upon students in our universities by some professors of physics, chemistry, biology, and psychology." They were perhaps remembering the words of Dr. Alfred North Whitehead, Professor of Philosophy in Harvard University: "Without religion nothing is really worth doing. It is hard to distract our minds from the deadly boredom of living a life that has lost its meaning because we have lost our faith." But above all things else these worldly men and women desired to know the peace that comes with citizenship in an earthly government authorized to determine what is truth eternal, and to recommend practices of duty and piety that merit everlasting peace as well as temporal content. They found themselves thinking of the pathetic figure of the man without a country and wondering were they themselves expatriates of the Kingdom of eternal verities. They saw the atheists of the world as restless brooders and sullen misanthropes, and prayed for rescue from the living death that is the lot of the hopeless who walk the highways of Time without a set destination.

The figure resting in peace in his church they saw to be a blessed contrast to their own heart's uneasiness. They saw his earthly remains as a symbol of the peace of soul that was his all through his earthly sojourn. They saw him wealthy in the lifelong possession of childhood's heart, at peace in hours of sorrow as well as in the multiplied occasions of happiness encountered along the highway that leads to Eternity's Port of Entry. They asked themselves, "Is it not necessary to have the endorsement of officials in a spiritual government of earth? One which we may present to the authorities who pass upon eligibility to enter the Kingdom of Peace Eternal?"

Amid those sorrowing multitudes, the poor man found peace in his soul as he contemplated the repose of a fellow pauper whose poverty was of his own choosing. The beggarman found a renewed sense of self-respect as he dwelt upon the life of the Prince of Christ's Kingdom who chose mendicancy as the profession which perpetuates Christ when the alms received are distributed to others in need of food, clothing, shelter. The doctor saw in the priest's remains the divine Physician's garment that gave healing to those who but touched in faith its hem. The lawyer heard once more the divine Barrister of Calvary whose charity for his destroyers found utterance in his plea to the Judge of Eternity's Supreme Court: "Father! Forgive them! They know not what they do!" The Indian Chief bows his head in prayer for the friend of the missions who opened up the Happy Hunting Grounds in the eternal courts of play, opened them up for himself and his tribesmen in exchange for the lands given to Christ's missionary crossbrearers.

The priesthood of Christ assigned to labor in the vineyard of America's democracy was represented in its plenitude at the sacred obsequies of a fellow in Holy Orders whose supreme moment in this life was, even as their own, the sacred instant when the Holy Ghost came upon him with the blessed words of annunciation uttered by the minister of Ordination's Sacrament: "Thou art a priest forever according to the Order of Melchizedek." Thirteen prelates of Archiepiscopal rank gloried with fifty-eight of their fellow Bishops that they were privileged to be in the presence of his holy remains still vested in his episcopal robes. They offered a prayer for him and to him as the Alter Christus who had passed from the Church Militant to the Church Triumphant. More than a thousand of his fellow priests found peace in the knowledge that his supreme joy was found in being, like themselves, a priest forever.

Christ, the Servant of the Servants of men, was represented in the Holy Father's emission, the Papal Delegate. Christ was a Real Presence in the sanctuary, the Prince of Peace, Who had called to His throne room the son whose life was an answered prayer—the prayer expressed in the words on his shield of office, "Stay with us, O Lord!"

May he rest in peace!